GREAT WAR BRITAIN

LONDON
Remembering 1914–18

STUART HALLIFAX

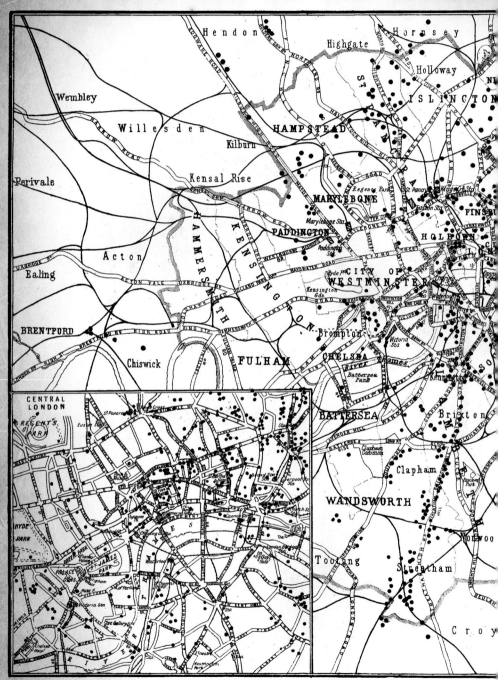

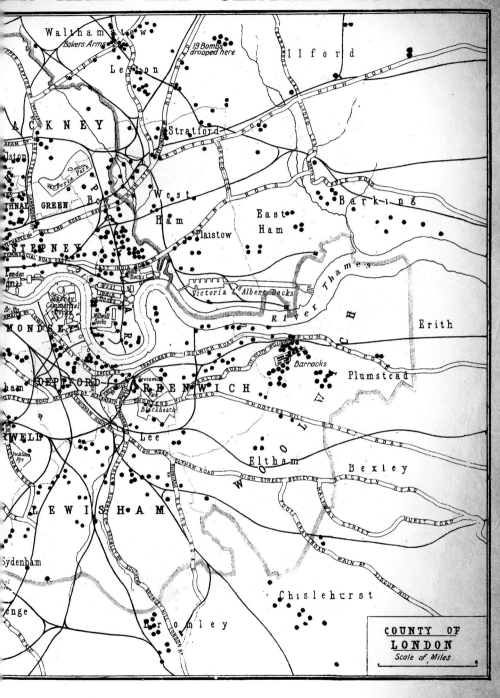

COUNTY OF
LONDON
Scale of Miles

First published 2014

The History Press
The Mill, Brimscombe Port
Stroud, Gloucestershire, GL5 2QG
www.thehistorypress.co.uk

British Library Cataloguing in Publication Data.
A catalogue record for this book is available from the British Library.

ISBN 978 0 7509 6046 5

Typesetting and origination by The History Press
Printed in Great Britain

CONTENTS

TIMELINE

1914

28 June

*Assassination of Archduke
Franz Ferdinand in Sarajevo*

4 August

*United Kingdom declares
war on Germany*

23 August

*Battle of Mons begins, the British
Expeditionary Force's first battle*

1 September

*Recruiting for British Army reaches
its peak: 24,814 recruits in London
in a week (186,000 nationwide)*

1915

21 April

*Second Battle of Ypres:
first German use of poison gas*

25 April

Allied landing at Gallipoli

7 May

Germans torpedo and sink the Lusitania

10 May

*Anti-German riots in London
and other British cities*

31 May

First German Zeppelin raid on London

25 September

*Battle of Loos: first British
use of poison gas*

20 December

*Allies finish their evacuation of
and withdrawal from Gallipoli*

1916

27 January
The Military Service Act: British government introduces conscription

21 February
Battle of Verdun commences

2 March
Conscription comes into force: unmarried men of military age deemed to have enlisted in the armed forces

31 May
Battle of Jutland

4 June
Russian Brusilov Offensive commences

1 July
First day of the Battle of the Somme, with 57,000 British casualties

2 September
Zeppelin shot down in flames over Cuffley, Hertfordshire, watched from all over London.

1917

19 January
Silvertown explosion

14 March
German withdrawal to the 'Hindenburg Line' commences

6 April
The United States declares war on Germany

9 April
Battle of Arras

13 June
First daylight air raid on London; 162 people killed, including children at North Street School, Poplar

31 July
Third Battle of Ypres (Passchendaele) commences

20 August
Third Battle of Verdun

26 October
Second Battle of Passchendaele

20 November
Battle of Cambrai

23 November
The bells of St Paul's Cathedral rung to celebrate the short-lived victory at Cambrai

1918

26 January

Food crisis at its peak: half a million
Londoners queue outside shops for food

25 February

Food rationing commences in
London and the Home Counties

3 March

Russia and the Central Powers
sign the Treaty of Brest-Litovsk:
Russia leaves the war

21 March

German Army launches its Spring
Offensive: Second Battle of the Somme

19 May

Last air raid on London

15 July

Second Battle of the Marne

8 August

Battle of Amiens, first stage of the
Hundred Days Offensive

27 September

Storming of the Hindenburg Line

8 November

Armistice negotiations commence

9 November

Kaiser Wilhelm II abdicates,
Germany is declared a Republic

11 November

Armistice Day, cessation of
hostilities on the Western Front

1919

19 July

Peace Day parade in central London
and celebrations across the city

1920

11 November

Permanent Cenotaph unveiled in
Whitehall and the Unknown Warrior
buried in Westminster Abbey

ACKNOWLEDGEMENTS

This book is drawn from research for my doctoral thesis on Essex during the Great War and for my ongoing blog on wartime London: greatwarlondon.wordpress.com

My thanks therefore go to those who have helped and supported me on those projects. To my parents for supporting me through my doctorate; particularly my mum, for proof-reading both my thesis and this book. To Adrian Gregory, for his supervision of my doctoral research. To Louise Peckett, for her support and patience while I have worked on the blog and this book. And to everyone with whom I have corresponded by email, through comments on blog posts, or in person, in the two years I have been writing my blog.

Thanks also to Mrs J.E. Sneddon for permission to quote from Alf Page's letters, and to the copyright holders of material quoted from the Imperial War Museum's archive, whom every effort has been made to contact.

The posters reproduced in this book come from the collection of the US Library of Congress; other images come from the *Illustrated War News*, wartime editions of the *Illustrated London News*, and items in the author's collection.

INTRODUCTION

On the eve of the Great War, London was the largest city the world had ever seen. It was the centre of the largest empire on Earth and of the financial world. Greater London was home to around 7 million men, women and children. The war that the United Kingdom entered on 4 August 1914 brought profound change to the British Empire, to the economic balance of the world, and to the lives of those millions of Londoners.

To tell in full the wartime experiences of this great and diverse city would take numerous volumes. Indeed there are already numerous histories of areas of London, ranging from those produced in the wake of the war itself, such as H.F. Morriss' *Bermondsey's 'Bit' in the Greatest War* and H. Keatley Moore and W.C. Berwick Sayers' *Croydon and the Great War*, to Tanya Britton's recent series of pamphlets on areas in the modern borough of Hillingdon, John King's *Grove Park in the Great War*, and numerous home front diaries and memoirs. A distinguished group of Great War academics, led by Professor Jay Winter, have produced two volumes of comparative history of London, Paris and Berlin entitled *Capital Cities at War*, which have been invaluable in the writing of this book. This short book attempts to give the reader a sense of both the broad changes and some of the countless individual experiences that war brought to London and its citizens. I hope that it will inspire Londoners to investigate the wartime stories of their neighbourhoods and boroughs.

Around a million men from London served in the armed forces of the Empire: they fought on all the battlefields, from Ypres to Archangel, and from the Dardanelles to Dar-es-Salaam. Women from the city served around the world in an increasing range of roles in the military. At home, people's lives and work were changed by the war: blackouts darkened the city; bombs were dropped from Zeppelins and aeroplanes onto London homes and businesses; factories shifted from peacetime production to manufacturing weapons and war equipment; soldiers flowed through the city on leave and to hospitals; women moved from domestic work to munitions factories, the service sector and transport; food became scarce and pubs closed early; and the lists of Londoners who would not return from the battle-fields grew ever longer.

These events could not have been foreseen. Even those who expected war in the years before 1914 could not have thought that the effort needed to win it could be maintained for fifty-two months at a cost to the Empire of a million lives and many millions of pounds.

In this volume we will see the war's impact on London. My focus is on the experience of the war in London, told through broad citywide trends, local and individual examples, and the first-hand accounts of people who lived in the city. A small number of these witnesses recur in these pages, including solicitor's wife Georgina Lee, restauranteur Mrs Hallie Eustace Miles, writer Mrs C.S. Peel, journalists Michael MacDonagh and Milton Valentine Snyder, nurse Vera Brittain, and soldiers including Jock Ashley and Len Smith. While I have included stories from across London, there is a slight bias towards central and eastern areas of the city, largely because the events of the war had a more observable impact in these areas: food queues grew and the aerial raiders visited there more often than West London and the suburbs.

When the war came, it crept up on Londoners and their contemporaries across Europe. Of greater concern in 1914 were tensions in Ireland, industrial unrest (after large strikes in 1912) and the campaign for women's suffrage, which had included arson and attacks on artworks in London's galleries.

The roots of the war can be traced back to the unification of Germany under Prussian leadership in the mid-nineteenth century, and its departure from Otto von Bismarck's policy of peace with Russia. As the new century began, international tensions were increasing, with suspicion between Germany and its neighbours France and Russia, who soon became allies. In 1904, Britain formed an *entente cordiale* with France that would see them stand together if one was attacked. This was soon followed by a similar agreement with Russia. It is debateable whether this alliance and that between Germany and Austria-Hungary helped to bring about the war, but they certainly shaped the responses of the major players in the Balkan Crisis of June and July 1914.

Unlike the more localised Balkan Wars in 1912 and 1913, the assassination of Archduke Franz Ferdinand, heir to the Austro-Hungarian throne, by a Serbian nationalist sparked off a chain of events that resulted in a continent-wide war. Serbia could not accept all of the demands made in Austria-Hungary's ultimatum following the assassination, and leaders in Vienna would not compromise. In the crisis that followed, Germany backed Austria-Hungary while Russia backed Serbia, bringing the prospect of the great alliances becoming involved. On 28 July, Austria-Hungary declared war on Serbia; Russia then began to mobilise its armed forces. Germany's leaders, fearing that Russian mobilisation would give them an advantage in the coming war, also mobilised. The German war plan, in recognition of the Franco-Russian alliance, was to knock France out of the war first, before Russia could get all of its forces in the field. To avoid French border defences, the plan took German troops through neutral Belgium. Whatever the United Kingdom's commitments to France and Russia, it was the invasion of 'poor little Belgium' from 3 August that brought British political and popular opinion behind involvement in the war. Each of the great powers was able to describe the war as defensive, which helped to secure popular support.

Watching the lamplighters at work in St James's Park on 3 August 1914, Foreign Secretary Sir Edward Grey famously remarked, 'The lamps are going out all over Europe; we shall not see them lit again in our lifetime.' London, the United Kingdom, and the British Empire were about to enter a war, the course of which none could predict. The effect of this conflict touched every home in the British Isles, and its impact has reverberated through the century since.

Stuart Hallifax
2014

1

LONDON GOES TO WAR

A huge crowd gathered outside Buckingham Palace to cheer King George V. Several thousand people – mainly young, middle class men – crowded around the Victoria Memorial and up Pall Mall in response to the news that Britain had entered 'the European War' on the side of France and 'poor little Belgium'. It was the evening of 4 August 1914 and Britain was at war with Germany. The scene provides the classic image of 1914 'war enthusiasm'.

It came as a shock to most people. Until late July, most saw the escalation of tensions in the Balkans as simply another local conflict. Georgina Lee, a solicitor's wife, wrote on 30 July that, 'Grave rumours of a possible terrible conflict of Nations are on everybody's lips and have been for some days.' The next day, the London Stock Exchange was closed in reaction to Russia's declaration of war against Austria-Hungary. On Saturday 1 August, Germany declared war on Russia and France mobilised its armed forces. The London correspondent of the *New York Times* reported that people now thought that the UK being 'drawn into a great European war … is now a probability rather than a possibility', but not yet inevitable. People's opinions about the war were divided: in Trafalgar Square, for example, a large anti-war rally passed a resolution in favour of international solidarity and peace on Sunday the 2nd; that evening the first crowds began to gather outside Buckingham Palace. The government extended Monday's bank holiday by two days to avoid a financial crisis when the stock markets reopened.

The German army's invasion of Belgium on 3 August convinced most of those who wavered over British involvement to accept that the nation would and should take part in the conflict. An ultimatum was sent to the Germans on Tuesday 4 August, due to expire at 11 p.m. (midnight in Berlin), demanding that they leave Belgian soil and honour its neutrality. As the moment approached, vast crowds gathered in Westminster; when Big Ben struck the fateful hour the people celebrated the declaration of war. Over the next few days, crowds gathered outside Buckingham Palace and in the West End and, according to the *New York Times*, 'Street vendors, shouting "Get your winning colors" [*sic*] were doing a rushing business, selling tiny Union Jacks, which the demonstrators wore on their coat lapels. There was also a brisk demand for French and Belgian flags.'

Elsewhere in London, crowds also gathered on 4 August to hear the news – there was of course no radio or television to inform them in their homes. In Fleet Street, crowds sang the British and French national anthems, but dispersed soon after the declaration of war was announced. In Ilford, according to the *Ilford Recorder*, 'Little knots of people gathered outside the local Territorial offices, and at various points all the way down the High-road from Chadwell Heath to the Clock Tower and railway station … awaiting the fateful declaration of war, and it was not until long after the momentous hour of midnight had struck that they began to disperse.'

The vast majority of people did not join these crowds, and those who did were often there seeking news rather than cheering on a war. While many people backed entering the war, most were not enthusiastic about what it might bring. In Croydon (according to the borough's war history *Croydon and The Great War*), 'our people braced themselves for their greatest war effort. There was bewilderment at first, but there was no panic. … Nor was there any war-fever, that enthusiasm which finds expression in flag-flapping, cheering, boasting, and the singing of patriotic songs. It was, as one acute observer remarked, "a war without a cheer"; it was too serious a matter.'

Germany's Anglophile ambassador, Prince Lichnowsky, leaving London in August 1914.

On Carlton House Terrace, near the Mall, people watched in a 'strange silence' as the German ambassador prepared to leave the embassy. According to the *Daily Mirror*, one man booed but was shushed by the crowd and led away by the police. The remaining crowd watched quietly as a workman removed the brass plaque bearing the German eagle from the outside of the building.

We should not get too carried away with an image of complete calm in London, however. Some celebrated, while others were panic-buying food in case supplies ran short or prices went up, with the predictable result that prices rose and shops ran low on goods. The dominant attitude was resolve or resignation, though: the war had to be fought, had to be put up with, and had to be won.

How long the public felt the conflict would last is very hard to tell. The phrase 'over by Christmas', so beloved of historians and novelists, was only rarely used in 1914. If people did expect a short war, the mid-August appeal for 100,000 men to join the army 'for three years or the duration' told them how long the nation's military leaders (especially Lord Kitchener, the Secretary of State for War) felt the war could last. Whether people thought it would last a few months, a year, or three years, few – if any – imagined the eventual scale of the conflict and the ways that it would affect life in London.

London Before the War

In August 1914, London could be described as being the centre of the world: it was the capital of an empire that included a fifth of the world's population and the centre of a system of trade that linked nations across the globe.

London had grown rapidly during the nineteenth century: from under 1 million people in 1801 to nearly 2 million in 1841 and over 4 million by 1891. By the start of the twentieth century, the growth of the city itself had almost stopped, but the urban area did not stop growing. While the county of London had reached 4.5 million in 1901, an 'outer ring' that made up the rest of Greater London grew from less than 1 million people in 1881 to 2 million in 1901. By 1911, it made up over a third of the 7.25 million people living in Greater London, the largest city on Earth.

The county of London – its new county hall on the South Bank was under construction in 1914 – was made up of the Cities of London and Westminster and twenty-eight metropolitan boroughs. The largest were Islington and Wandsworth, each with over 300,000 inhabitants; Lambeth, Camberwell and Stepney also had more than a quarter of a million inhabitants each. Most metropolitan boroughs had at least 85,000 inhabitants, with Chelsea and Holborn among the smallest, with only 66,000 and 50,000 residents respectively.

The outer ring of Greater London comprised: the whole of Middlesex (1.1 million people in 1911), which included Hendon, Ealing, Edmonton, Willesden and Finchley; areas of Surrey containing 500,000 people, including Croydon, Wimbledon, Barnes, Richmond and Epsom; Kent districts, including Beckenham, Bexley, Bromley and Erith, containing 172,000 people; the urban areas of south-west Essex containing Barking, East Ham, West Ham, Ilford, Walthamstow and Leyton, with over 800,000 residents; and an area of Hertfordshire with 55,000 inhabitants, including Watford, Barnet and Bushey.

Over such a broad area and so many people, there was of course a wide variety of labour and living conditions. Many of the Victorian suburbs that encircled the city in the 'outer ring' were home to clerks and professionals working in Central London, while the area in the docks either side of the Thames in East London included large numbers of dockers and warehousemen. East and West Ham were also home to a large amount of heavy industry (helpfully, the London rules on factory emissions did not apply over the River Lea in Essex), while the Royal Arsenal was situated on the other side of the river, at Woolwich.

Just under half of the 1.4 million male workers in the county of London worked in the service sector, and 12 per cent in transport (on rail, roads and the river, including the Port of London Authority). Another 16.6 per cent worked in commerce and 2.7 per cent in banking and insurance alone. Soldiers, sailors and marines made up another 15,000 workers. A third of London's workers were women, primarily in service (over 200,000 domestic servants, plus 35,000 laundry workers and 30,000 charwomen) but a large number worked in the clothing industry, as well as an increasing number employed as clerks (32,000), teachers (18,000) and nurses (16,000). Two of the largest cross-London employers were the London County Council (LCC) and the Metropolitan Police. The latter broadly covered the area of Greater London, while the council was for the county itself. Both organisations employed large numbers of ex-servicemen.

London Regiment battalions appealed directly to men to join their ranks, in this case for clerks to join the London Rifle Brigade. (Library of Congress, LC-USZC4-10960)

As well providing men for the regular army and housing many reservists (ex-servicemen who could be called up in an emergency), London was home to one of the few regiments of the British Army entirely made up of part-time soldiers – members of the Territorial Force, created in 1908 out of the old militias and volunteer corps of the previous century. The London Regiment had twenty-six battalions, including London-wide units such at the London Rifle Brigade, the Rangers and Queen Victoria's Rifles, those for men with shared backgrounds and jobs like the London Scottish and the Civil Service Rifles, and those for areas, such as Blackheath and Woolwich, Hackney, and Camberwell (the First Surrey Rifles). There were also artillery and medical units, and the Honourable Artillery Company, which (despite its name) was an infantry unit based in the City of London. The Middlesex, Essex, East Surrey and West Surrey Regiments also had London-based territorial battalions. Although it had no Territorial Force battalions, the Royal Fusiliers were the 'City of London Regiment'.

The Call to Arms

As soon as war was declared, the number of men volunteering for the armed forces overwhelmed the recruiting offices. Tens of thousands of Territorials and Reservists were reported for duty, but the more startling sight was that of civilians queuing for hours to join up. At first there were too few recruiting offices to cope with the enormous demand and the crowds became enormous – especially around the Central London recruiting office at Great Scotland Yard, off Whitehall. London Regiment battalions had their own recruiting offices, which were also overcrowded. City clerk Bernard Brookes waited for two or three hours on Buckingham Palace Road on 7 August to join the Queen's Westminster Rifles (16th Londons): 'After much swearing outside the building, we were "sworn in"'.

This 'rush to the colours' was an extraordinary increase on peacetime recruiting; within eleven days, more men had come forward to join the army than in any of the previous four years: almost 39,000 men (nearly 10,000 in London alone). New

Alfred Leete's famous image for the magazine London Opinion *summed up Lord Kitchener's call to arms. (Library of Congress, LC-USZC4-3858)*

19

G. R.

"WE are fighting for a worthy purpose, and we shall not lay down our arms until that purpose has been fully achieved."

THE KING

MEN OF THE EMPIRE

To ARMS!

GOD SAVE THE KING!

A typical parliamentary recruiting poster of autumn 1914, before the picture posters that characterised the later recruiting campaign. (Library of Congress, LC-USZC4-10872)

recruiting offices were established across the capital: on 7 August, *The Times* reported new offices opening in Camberwell, Islington, Battersea, Fulham, and Marylebone. The head-quarters of German shipping firm Hamburg-Amerika on Cockspur Street also became a recruiting office. By 30 August, over 168,000 men had joined the army, including over 29,000 in London. An even greater recruiting boom was about to begin, though – well beyond anything seen before in the nation's history.

On 23 August, the British Expeditionary Force (BEF) first encountered the German Army at Mons in Belgium, only a few miles from Waterloo, where British and German forces had defeated Napoleon in 1815. Among the men who encountered the Germans at Mons was Lance Corporal Ernest Stretton from Islington; called up from the reserves in August 1914, he went straight into battle and was killed at Mons. The BEF suffered heavily in the fighting there and in the retreat to the Marne that followed it, but the Allies' fighting retreat eventually brought the German offensive to a halt. Another reservist, William Hurcombe from Walworth, arrived in France on 26 August with the 20th Hussars and entered straight into the retreat from Mons; he survived that battle and numerous others through the rest of the war.

News soon got back to Britain about the losses at Mons. On 30 August, a report appeared in *The Times* stressing the threat to the very existence of the BEF and the need for more soldiers: recruiting rates for the army immediately rocketed. Men came forward in droves to help defend their nation. Helpfully, the timing also coincided with the end of harvest in rural areas and the peak of wartime unemployment in London;

the recruitment boom also included those men who had earlier decided to join but first needed to sort out their personal affairs. The combination of these factors, public pressure and increased pro-recruiting rhetoric and speeches, brought in 4,000 recruits in London on 1 September (the next weekday after *The Times'* report was published), more than double the rate of any previous day. In the first week of September, 24,814 men enlisted in London. Nationally, over 186,000 men joined up that week – more than in the whole of August, with over 33,000 on both the 4th and 5th of that month. Between 4 August and an increase in the height requirements on 11 September, 463,456 men joined up, including 67,276 in London.

A hopeful recruiting poster from the first winter of the Great War. (Library of Congress, LC-USZC4-10946)

This great rush of men came before the big national recruiting campaigns. In fact, it was in the wake of the steep decline in recruiting after 11 September that the national campaign really got going: London's weekly enlistment rate fell from 15,000 to under 5,000 three weeks later (and the national rate fell from 100,000 to 15,000). The Parliamentary Recruiting Committee (PRC) – a national body with branches in every constituency – was formed at the height of the boom and began their work as enlistment declined, with their famous posters coming mainly in 1915. The most widely-known 1914 recruiting image is the 'Kitchener Wants You' poster, which was not in fact an official recruiting poster, nor was it very widely used at the time. The image was created by Alfred Leete (who was later responsible for some memorable London Underground posters) for the magazine *London Opinion*; featured on the cover of the 5 September issue, the magazine then sold it as a poster a few weeks later. Despite its later success, including being copied for a US Army poster in 1917, the Leete 'Kitchener' poster was more an encapsulation of the power of the call to arms and the celebrity status of Lord Kitchener than a widespread recruiting tool of 1914.

The role of women in men's enlistment was varied and ambiguous. The trend of young women giving white feathers to young men out of uniform was not as widespread as popular memory suggests, but it was very real and it was more prevalent in London than elsewhere: it was much easier to tell a stranger to go and fight than to demand the same of a lover, son or brother. Henry Allingham had attempted to join up in August but was told in no uncertain terms by his mother that he was to stay at home, which he did until her death in 1915. Similarly, lawyer A. Stuart Dolden's parents were not impressed when he opted to leave his new job at Liverpool Street to join the London Scottish.

In October, 136,600 men joined up, compared with 462,900 in September (30,600 in London compared to 67,700). A greater effort was needed to increase enlistments: the PRC began to plan its national recruiting campaign and the rhetoric against 'slackers' increased. Its first posters were straightforward restatements in bold text of the appeal for men by the king and Lord Kitchener. Up to that point, the main tool of recruiters was the recruiting meeting – events set up by local councils and other organisations or individuals to encourage young men to join up. At football matches, placards called for enlistment and recruiters harangued the civilian spectators. Journalist Michael MacDonagh saw men outside a Chelsea match in December wearing sandwich boards bearing 'such questions as "Are you forgetting there's a War on?" "Your Country Needs You", and "Be Ready to Defend your Home and Women from the German Huns". So far as I could notice, little attention was given to these skeletons at the feast.'

The War Office effectively outsourced a lot of recruiting to groups who wanted to help with the war effort. This resulted in new units being formed of men from similar locations and backgrounds, widely known as 'pals' units. The first of these was the Stockbrokers' Battalion (10th Royal Fusiliers), formed in August 1914. Public Schools battalions were formed in the Royal Fusiliers and the Middlesex Regiment in early September. The 17th

Middlesex, created in December 1914, was the 1st Footballers' battalion, which players joined in large numbers (including a large group from Clapton Orient), countering accusations that footballers were shirking their duty. A broader Sportsmen's battalion of the Royal Fusiliers had been formed in September and a second in November. The trend persisted well beyond the recruiting boom and was used in the attempts to revive the feeling of late summer 1914; a Bankers' battalion (26th Royal Fusiliers) was created in July 1915, while the East Ham battalion (32nd Royal Fusiliers) was only formed in October 1915. Other boroughs had got in on the act earlier, including Kensington (22nd Royal Fusiliers) in September 1914, with Shoreditch and Islington battalions (20th and 21st Middlesex) formed in May 1915. These 'pals' units were not restricted to infantry, though: artillery brigades were formed in Camberwell, Deptford, East Ham, Fulham, Hampstead, West Ham and Wimbledon, and by the Thames Ironworks.

In October, Lord Curzon, a former Viceroy of India and future Foreign Secretary, gave a speech at Harrow School. The *Manchester Guardian* reported that he told the audience that he 'was perfectly shocked when he read in the papers of people talking about the war being over by Christmas … In his judgement more than one Christmas would pass before our soldiers returned.' This was the only time that a prominent British politician (or military commander) publicly acknowledged the idea of the war ending by Christmas – and he used it to admonish men for not enlisting under that misapprehension, rather than to promise an early victory!

THE ARMED FORCES IN 1914–18

THE ARMY
The Regular Army

Reservists (mainly ex-soldiers): liable to be called on in emergencies

Territorial Force: part-time soldiers originally intended for home defence but encouraged to volunteer for 'imperial service' once the war began

'Service' battalions of the New Army: formed for active service in response to Lord Kitchener's call to arms

ROYAL NAVY
The Regular Navy

Royal Naval Reserve/ Royal Naval Volunteer Reserve

ROYAL AIR FORCE
Formed in 1918 from

- Royal Flying Corps, an army unit established in 1912
- Royal Naval Air Service, formed in 1914

Doing Their Bit at Home

The first response of many people who could not enlist because of their age or gender was to do something to help the men at the front – giving their time, money or resources. As we will see later, many wealthy residents of London gave up rooms or houses to be used as military hospitals. Londoners of all classes also gave money to charity campaigns, the biggest of which in 1914 was the 'National Relief Fund', launched by the Prince of Wales in early August. After a year it had raised £5.5 million for the relief of civilian distress caused by the war, some of which was distributed to ease wartime distress, mostly to help the dependents of men who had enlisted that suffered from a severe delay in sorting out separation allowances.

Others volunteered their time. For men who were too old and boys who were too young (and arguably men who did not want to serve overseas), there were local defence groups formed in the early months of the war. These were later grouped together under the title Volunteer Training Corps. Others volunteered to help the police by becoming special constables; their main roles were enforcing lighting restrictions, guarding vulnerable buildings from German sabotage, and – later on – helping to keep crowds of angry civilians in order. Women were more constrained in what they could offer; they could nurse and many did, but when a group of women volunteered early on as drivers they were snootily sent home. A much more acceptable female contribution was knitting: groups of women gathered to knit gloves, scarves and balaclavas for the men at the front and, importantly, to feel useful. Patterns were published in newspapers for these and other 'comforts' that people could make for soldiers.

DORA

At the outset of the war, Parliament passed the first Defence of the Realm Act; that Act (known by the more innocuous acronym DORA) gave the government incredibly broad powers over individuals and businesses. By November 1914, the Act and its successors enabled the trial by court martial of anyone deemed to be communicating with or assisting the enemy, endangering the security of the armed forces, or spreading 'false reports or reports likely to cause disaffection to His Majesty or to interfere with the success of His Majesty's forces'. The government could also take control of any factory or workshop manufacturing military equipment or munitions. The gradual militarisation of Britain followed over the next four years, with blackouts, controls on the movements of non-British residents, restrictions on the sale of food and drink, and controls on people's employment.

The Enemy in our Midst

People's attitudes towards Germans changed from the very start of the war. German citizens and German-born Britons who had lived peacefully in communities for years suddenly became potential enemies, feared and hated. Aliens (foreign citizens) had to register with the police and were restricted to their local areas – journeys of more than 5 miles could only be made with the permission of the police.

Official actions like registration and the deployment of soldiers and boy scouts to defend strategically important sites (including bridges and reservoirs) helped to fuel a spy-mania across Britain. Citizens saw spies everywhere, especially when they heard a Germanic accent.

MINORITY COMMUNITIES IN LONDON
Although not quite the multicultural city it has become a century later, London was home to communities of people from across the world. There was a thriving German community, with German churches and societies across the capital, and many more Germans who had assimilated into their local communities. Almost 27,300 Germans lived in the county of London in 1911; another 3,762 lived in Middlesex and 1,970 in Essex (mainly within Greater London). Around 8,500 Austrians also lived in London and Middlesex. They were not the largest migrant group, as a large number of Russian Jews had come to Britain in the decades before the war to escape the anti-Semitic Tsarist regime there; over 64,000 settled in London and Middlesex. There were also large communities from other European countries, including France and Italy (15,000 and 12,000 people respectively). The number of non-European immigrants and their descendants was much smaller, but there were people of Indian and African-Caribbean descent, and a sizeable Chinese community, particularly in Limehouse.

A pre-war boom in invasion literature had prepared people for these fears. Erskine Childers' *The Riddle of the Sands* was the most popular in the genre, but William Le Queux's *The Invasion of 1910* must have struck a chord in London, depicting a German invasion with fighting in the heart of London and a massacre at St Pancras. The book was serialised in the *Daily Mail* in 1906 and advertised in London's streets by men dressed as Prussian soldiers. A German invasion, with spies lurking among the population of London, was not beyond people's imagination.

One of the strangest incidents of 1914 must have been the departure of the Austro-Hungarian ambassador in mid-August. As he passed through Paddington station, a group of Austrians on the platform began to sing their national anthem. Understandably indignant at their enemy's anthem being sung in London, a British crowd promptly struck up 'God Save the King'. The station was thus filled with the discordant sound of two belligerent nations' national anthems.

Public opinion became more vehement in late August when – alongside the news that the survival of the BEF was threatened – there came stories of German 'frightfulness' in France and Belgium. Civilians were fired on by the German Army, libraries had been burned, and local dignitaries taken hostage by the advancing Germans. Alongside the true stories of brutality came salacious rumours of bayoneted babies and women's breasts being cut off by bloodthirsty Huns: these tales of horror were elaborated on by wounded British soldiers and Belgian refugees arriving in London. The stories and exaggerations whipped British public opinion up into a fury and seemed to confirm that Britain was at threat from a brutal German race that would stop at nothing to crush its enemies. With this racial view of the war, Germans living in Britain were deemed no less to blame than the soldiers who had killed Belgian civilians.

Journalist Michael MacDonagh observed in October that:

A large section of the public continue to suffer from the first bewildering shock of war. Their nerves are still jangling, and they are subject to hallucinations.

They seem to be enveloped in a mysterious darkness, haunted by goblins in the form of desperate German spies, and they can find no light or comfort afforded them by Press or Government.

In the absence of reported incidents of espionage in the press, rumours of spies and sabotage filled the void, including a woman who had apparently captured four German spies dressed as nuns on a bus in Brixton. In November, though, a real spy – Carl Hans Lody – was caught, tried at the Middlesex Guildhall, and executed in the Tower of London. The very small number of real cases no doubt fuelled still further the fevered imaginations of the population.

German spy Carl Hans Lody on trial in Middlesex Guildhall.

Hostilities could result from these fears, as reported in the *Barking Advertiser* in October:

Several exciting scenes took place in Leyton on Saturday night, when demonstrations were made outside shops owned by Germans. Owing to regulations now in force the streets were in semi-darkness. The first outbreak occurred outside the shop of a pork butcher in High-street. It was stated that as a man was leaving the shop with meat another man came up and knocked the meat out of his hand to the ground, saying, 'You ought to be ashamed to trade with that —— German.' A crowd quickly gathered and became so large that trams and other vehicles had trouble in passing. Uncomplimentary remarks were made about Germans in general, and the proprietor was called upon to close his shop and put his lights out. After a time the police came on the scene and requested the people on the pavement to move on. The crowd congregated on the other side of the street and hooted, and shouted to the proprietor to close his premises. The crowd proceeded further down the street and demonstrated outside the premises of a baker. They next paid attention to another baker's establishment, where they cheered, jeered, and sang 'Rule Britannia'. Similar demonstrations were made outside a German's shop in High-road, Leytonstone.

Life became increasingly difficult for Germans living in Britain. Richard Noschke, a German who had lived in East Ham for over twenty years, was dismissed by his long-term employer in December 1914. When he wrote to them later, they maintained their view that all Germans were to blame for the war and the 'frightfulness' of the German armed forces. His next employer did not let on to others that Noschke was German, but fired him after a few months for fear of the impact on his business if people did find out. By then, very few firms would employ a German and it was only after being confused for a Russian that Noschke was able to find work.

Lamps are Dimmed all over London

'Lighting orders' issued during 1914 restricted the use of street-lamps and the display of lights in the windows of shops and houses. Across London, windows had to be blacked out and street lamps either extinguished or shaded. People had to either make their way around in the dark or carry an electric torch – although some districts banned these. By November 1914, there were calls by London councils for more lighting to counter the dangers of the darkened streets.

Michael MacDonagh described the darkness of the city at night that month:

Very few of the street lamps were burning, and these were so masked that their light fell only at their feet. As I walked … to my office I could not catch even the faintest or most distant sound of traffic … The town clocks are silent and at night their dials are not lighted.

Big Ben has ceased to sound the quarters and the hours since the middle of last month. So all the mighty heart of London was still. But the sky was being lit up and pierced by flashing searchlights.

MP Christopher Addison complained in his diary that the streets of Westminster were so dark that he had to feel for the kerb with his feet since he could not see it. In April 1915, the Commissioner for Police suggested painting the kerbs white; it was for councils to decide and some (including St Marylebone) felt that it was unnecessary, as the days were getting longer anyway. When the suggestion came again in November, St Marylebone had already begun work whitening the kerbs.

Despite the blackout, there was still some light. Hallie Miles described Central London in late 1914:

Nearly all the lights in the shop windows are shaded with different colours, and these many coloured lights are reflected in the street and on to the pavements; when there is rain the puddles are turned into glorified iridescent pools, and the pavements and roads are like rainbows. The shop windows too, with the coloured lights cast down upon the goods displayed, look very mysterious and almost fairy-like. So we have our compensations.

2

THE WAR SPIRIT

Anti-German Sentiment

We have already seen how Germans became hate figures in August 1914. Following the army's brutality in France and Belgium, the German navy reinforced their nation's brutal reputation when, in November and December 1914, warships shelled Great Yarmouth and then Hartlepool, Scarborough and Whitby. The deaths of children in these raids painted the Germans as 'babykillers' and beneath contempt. This was apparently confirmed when a German submarine sank the ocean liner RMS *Lusitania* off the coast of Ireland on 7 May 1915, killing 1,201 people, including 94 children. Riots flared up across London and other cities from 10 May; London's riots occurred primarily, but not solely, in the East End, with its large German, Russian and Eastern European immigrant populations.

The *Hackney and Kingsland Gazette* summed up events well on 14 May:

TAKE UP THE
SWORD OF JUSTICE

Throughout the whole of North London on Wednesday night the premises of Germans and others suspected of being of German nationality were the object of violent demonstrations on the part of enraged crowds, who, by smashing windows and doing all the damage possible, vented their indignation at the brutality of the German methods of warfare, which culminated in the sinking of the 'Lusitania'. Although the outbreaks were not of so serious a nature as those occurring in the East-end of London and at Liverpool … they were nevertheless of a most determined and widespread character.

The newspaper went on to describe one particular attack:

The angriest demonstration in this district took place outside the bakery establishment of Joseph Engel, facing Median-road, in Lower Clapton-road, where a crowd of several thousands collected and a constant volley of bricks and stones was directed against the shop. … A number of women first began to collect at the corner of Median-road, and about nine o'clock, when the crowd had swelled to goodly proportions, and assumed a threatening attitude, a woman suddenly came forward and flung a half-brick. It struck the plate-glass window full in the centre, and the crash was greeted with an outburst of cheering. It was followed by the throwing of other missiles which almost entirely demolished the remaining plate glass. One or two of the upstairs windows were also broken … Aid was rendered to the ordinary police by the special constabulary, and a cordon was eventually formed and the crowd was pressed back. The latter, however, then took long-range shots, and in this way the interior of the shop was more or less ruined. The shop fronts of Mr. Frank, butcher, and the Lion Hat Company, adjoining Mr. Engel's, were both damaged, and the windows were broken by stones.

The same crowd also attacked nearby bakers' and butchers' shops 'which were not ostensibly English'. As across East London, it did not matter to the crowd whether the shop owner was German or naturalised, or often if they were actually Russian Poles. The police, aided by special constables, struggled and all too often failed to control the mobs. Sylvia Pankhurst witnessed a crowd beating a woman until she lay bloody and unconscious in the street; only at that point did the police step in. A pork butcher's shop in Upton Park was completely ransacked, with the stock and even the linoleum flooring stolen. Pankhurst wrote of a riot in Bethnal Green:

> Looting continued with impunity for days, incited and organised by certain jingo factions. Men unknown in the district, with hatchets on their shoulders, marched through Bethnal Green Road, Green Street, the Roman Road to the very end. Wherever a shop had a German name over it they stopped and hacked down the shutters and broke the glass. Then crowds of children rushed in and looted. When darkness fell and the police made no sign, men and women joined the sack.

The next week's *Essex County Chronicle* reported that there were 110 cases before the magistrates at West Ham and 38 in East Ham as a result of the riots.

In some places, prominent locals stepped in to protect the victims of riots: a Leyton councillor headed off a crowd in front of the house of a man named Schmidt, telling them that two of Schmidt's sons were serving in the British Army. Many shopkeepers posted notices with similar messages in their windows but often were not as lucky as Mr Schmidt.

Perhaps predictably, the riots spread well beyond German-owned and even foreign-named properties. A pub owned by a Scotsman called Strachan was ransacked; as journalist Michael MacDonagh wrote: 'In the opinion of the British in the East End, it is better that a Scotsman with a German-looking name, or an Irishman with a German-sounding voice, should suffer (both being colourable imitations of Germans) than that a genuine German should escape.' In the docks, as the riots continued, the mob reportedly attacked shops whose owners had been kind to 'blacklegs' during the 1912 dock strike; existing community tensions were given an opportunity for release under the guise of attacking the Germans.

There was widespread support for the motivation behind the anti-German riots, if not the violent methods. Georgina Lee wrote in her diary on 11 May, 'At John's Wood … A German was being molested, and his house attacked. He had six carrier pigeons there. The police had to protect him. Many such scenes occur everywhere and thank goodness the people are fighting this danger themselves, instead of waiting for the Government to take slow measures.' (Pigeons were known accessories of espionage and their ownership by 'enemy aliens' was banned.) A few days later, as the riots continued, she wrote, 'Why, I ask, are there such hundreds of German butchers and bakers in London?' Lee was not the first, or the last, person to question the continued presence of Germans (or German-born Britons) in their midst. In July 1915, Southwark Council passed a resolution calling for the internment of all Germans, whether aliens or naturalised Britons. An Anti-German Union (from 1916, the British Empire Union) was set up to campaign for internment and against the resumption of trade with Germany after the war.

After the riots, rumours flew that certain individuals were Germans or spies. Herbert Lengman in Plaistow even placed an advert in the *East Ham Recorder* offering £100 to anyone who could prove that he was not 'a true Englishman'. It was the second time Lengman had done this, and he was far from the only one. Grove Park bakers Mr and Mrs Anderson had earlier offered £100 to anyone who could prove they were of German descent, or £10 to anyone uncovering the source of the rumour. J. Lyons & Co. successfully sued Lipton's, the iced tea makers, for libel in 1914 over claims that Lyon's was German and that 'by purchasing their commodities the public is assisting the enemies of Great Britain'. Some families changed their Germanic names to make themselves appear more British, much to the chagrin of the jingoistic factions, who feared this was a ruse for spies. This concern does not seem to have extended to the Royal Family's name change, from Saxe-Coburg and Gotha to the more acceptable Windsor, in 1917.

Across the country, German and Austrian men of military age were detained in internment camps from late 1914. In the wake of the *Lusitania* riots, this policy was significantly expanded. Observers who did not necessarily see these men as evil nonetheless thought that it was best to intern them for their own protection. Some German Londoners ended up interned in a former factory on Carpenter's Road, next to the railway tracks in Stratford. Here, 750 men endured a ruthless regime run by the military authorities. Richard Noschke was lucky enough to obtain a job in the camp's garden, but found that anti-German feeling continued outside the barbed wire:

> The railway was running along side the piece of garden and constant trains passing by, filled with soldiers who on every occasion used the most fearful language and drawing theyr [*sic*] swords and threatening us in a most frightfull [*sic*] manner, and if they could have got out of theyr train, I am sure they would have murdered every one of us. Even so call Gentlemen in first-class compartment shook theyr fist at us when the train passed by, and used the very essence of expression. On one side of the yard was a high wall, and carmen [driving horse-drawn vehicles] sitting high up on theyr seats could see quite clearly inside the yard but on nearly every occasion they spit at us and used such swearing language which was horrifining [*sic*].

Others, including Noschke himself after two years in Stratford, were interned in much better conditions in Alexandra Palace. Approximately 17,000 people stayed at Alexandra Palace at some point in the war. There were two other civilian camps in London: at Holloway and Cornwallis Road in Islington, as well as military prisoner of war camps at Edmonton, Eastcote and Feltham; Kensington Olympia was also used temporarily.

Like Georgina Lee, many were baffled by the continued presence of Germans in London. Mr Lindsey Johnson of the Anti-German Union was a particularly prominent campaigner against their presence: in September 1915, he disguised himself as a priest to infiltrate and disrupt a German Lutheran service in Forest Hill. In October he turned up at a German service in Brompton. He was still active in 1917, breaking up a German service in Walthamstow. Around the same time, rumours spread in Walthamstow that the local 'Pluton Works' factory prioritised Germans over Britons in their air-raid shelter; unfortunately, the company's reassurance that Germans and Britons were treated alike simply prompted further questions about why they employed Germans at all.

In early 1918, Westminster City Council backed Southwark in 'urging the London County Council to remove the names of streets having German origin or reference and to substitute Colonial names therefor' (some streets were renamed: Berlin Road in Catford is now Canadian Avenue). That summer, the mayors of London boroughs called for action, passing a motion 'that all enemy aliens and naturalised subjects of enemy origin, of the age of 18 years and upwards, should be forthwith interned, and should remain interned during the continuance of the war'.

In August 1918, a 'monster rally' took place in Hyde Park, accompanied by bands, banners, soldiers and trade union contingents (wartime Britons liked their rallies to be 'monster'). The nationwide petition it delivered to Downing Street was said to be 2 miles long and contain 1.2 million names. By that time, the government were already responding to public demands by reviewing the cases of 6,000 Germans, thought to be the whole population still at large in Britain after earlier internments and the repatriation of women and older men (including Richard Noschke, who returned to Germany in February 1918). Michael MacDonagh was told that 300 more Germans had recently been interned in London by the time of the rally and petition. All in all, London – and Britain more generally – was not a comfortable place for people of German descent in 1914–18.

The Search for Volunteers

After the recruiting boom of August and September 1914, the government and local bigwigs tried their best to rekindle the emotions of those weeks and increase pressure on those young men who had not enlisted then to come forward. The national PRC produced 20 million leaflets and 2 million posters by the end of March 1915 and eventually printed 12.5 million posters of 164 designs, aimed at bringing men into the armed forces. Local committees also produced leaflets and held meetings and rallies.

Many of the PRC's posters have since achieved great fame or notoriety. Posters with messages such as 'Women of Britain Say – Go!' and 'What did you do in the Great War, Daddy?' recalled the reasons that many men had enlisted in 1914: a sense of duty or shame. But they were not as effective as is often assumed: they failed to counter the decline in recruiting that continued throughout most of the year. The main spikes in enlistment in 1915 came in response to the sinking of the *Lusitania* and at the point in late 1915 when men were told that if they didn't join up as

Royal Horse Guards machine-gunners training on a golf course near London.

Recruiting meetings were held in London throughout late 1914 and 1915.
(Library of Congress, LC-USZC4-11044)

The threat of Zeppelin attacks on London was used to urge men to join the armed forces. (Library of Congress, LC-USZC4-10972)

volunteers they would be conscripted. The most widely reproduced PRC recruiting poster during the war was one that recalled the sinking of the *Lusitania*, calling on men to 'Take up the sword of justice' in response to this latest act of 'frightfulness'.

Recruiting meetings and marches and the creation of local units continued – alongside the poster campaign. These did bring in more men, but suffered from the inherent problem that men who did not plan to enlist were not likely to attend a recruiting event. In October 1915, a 'monster' recruiting march made its way through London: five columns of soldiers coming in from the suburbs

The execution of nurse Edith Cavell by the Germans further hardened British attitudes, providing another spur to enlist.

and converging in the city. Michael MacDonagh followed one: 'I accompanied one of the columns on its entire march through the City, along Holborn and Oxford Street, and up Tottenham Court Road to Camden Town. "Wake up, London!" was the motto of the rally. It certainly caused a great stir everywhere.' Recruiting sergeants called for young men in the crowd to enlist. Despite the crowd's 'cries of execration hurled at young fellows who turned away, as most of them did, from the recruiting-sergeants', wrote MacDonagh, the march did not inspire hoards of recruits: 'The reports from the various recruiting stations in the evening was that the response to the rally was "normal."'

The Path to Compulsion

From 1914 there were calls for conscription, lamenting the nation's failure to heed pre-war calls for compulsory National Service. Through 1915, declining recruitment and the military's demand for more men brought conscription ever closer. The state

Men 'attesting' under the Derby Scheme were issued with 'armlets' to symbolise their 'willingness to serve' if needed.

intervened directly in the recruiting process in August 1915, ordering local authorities to compile a National Register of every man and woman aged between 15 and 65. The Register confirmed that a large number of military-aged men had not joined up.

Posters urged men to enlist or attest voluntarily before conscription began on 2 March 1916. (Library of Congress, LC-USZC4-11021)

In an almost stereotypically British compromise, the last phase of voluntary recruiting was in fact a form of voluntary conscription. The 'Derby Scheme' (named after the Director General for Recruiting, the 17th Earl of Derby) saw men on the National Register aged 18 to 40 canvassed and asked to either enlist in the armed forces or 'attest their willingness to serve' when called for. Those who attested were given an 'armlet' to wear to show that they were 'willing to serve'. Men were promised the opportunity to appeal against being called if they were essential at home or in their work, and the myth was peddled that it was only as Derby attestees that men would be able to appeal.

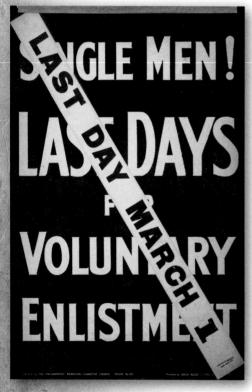

During the last days of the scheme, there was a rush to attest, which the newspapers portrayed as akin to the recruiting boom of 1914. It could also be seen as a rush *not* to join up, with men confident that they would be exempted from service if they attested. Married men could feel safe from the call after the government promised that single men would be called for first, leading a satirist in the *East Ham Collegian* magazine to define the Derby armlet as 'a badge worn by married men … to show their sympathy with the principle of "Single Men First".'

In December 1915, it was announced that 2.19 million men had attested under the Derby Scheme up to mid-October; another 115,000 had enlisted and 230,000 were rejected as unfit. Attestees' National Registration cards were stamped to show that they had stated their 'willingness to serve'. Of the nation's attestees, 750,000 were 'starred' (meaning that their jobs were protected as vital to the war effort), leaving 538,000 single and 895,000 married men available to be called up, but another 2 million who had not joined up or attested, including 650,000 single men. This was not enough attestees to keep the army going, though: conscription was on the way.

Conscription

On 27 January 1916, Parliament passed the first Military Service Act, which deemed every unmarried man aged 18 to 40 to have enlisted in the armed forces and liable to be called to

A strange sight in a suburban street: new recruits marching in their gas masks.

The first 'Derby' recruits report for duty at Whitehall, 1916.

serve. Identifying an obvious loophole that might have seen a sudden rush of marriages, the Act referred to the man's status in November 1915. The call-up started on 2 March 1916, heralded by posters, on Town Halls and around the base of Nelson's Column, encouraging last-minute volunteers and attestees: 'Will you March too, or wait till March 2?' The last man to attest was reportedly a Mr S. Salomans from Stepney, at 11.55 p.m. on 1 March 1916.

It soon became clear that single men were not sufficient. Their Derby 'groups' and conscript 'classes' (cohorts to which men were assigned by year of birth) were called up more quickly than anyone expected and it became obvious that married attested men would be called up. This caused outrage, due to the government appearing to break their pledge that all single men would go first, and the apparent punishment of those married men who had attested, who would be called before the 'shirkers' who had stayed back. The obvious riposte to this was that they should not have attested their willingness to serve if they were not willing to serve. Nonetheless, there were 'married men's rallies' at Tower Hill and across the country, at which attested married men demanded the conscription of all single men and the extension of conscription to include un-attested married men. This extension came with another Military Service Act on 25 May.

Under the Derby Scheme 2,086 local tribunals had been set up nationwide to hear the appeals of men who did not feel that they should be called up because the resulting domestic or business hardship would be too extreme, that they were indispensable to their employers, they did work of 'national importance', or they were unfit for military service. From March, they also heard conscripts' appeals, including those based on conscientious objection to military service.

Tribunals were set up by borough and district councils and were made up primarily of local councillors. In urban areas, trade union representatives were often included. There was also a Military Representative (from 1917 referred to as a 'National Service' Representative), who assessed each appeal from the military's perspective, very often arguing that the man should be called up. If a man, his employer, or the Military Representative disagreed with the local tribunal's decision, they could take the appeal to a county tribunal – for London this meant the County of London Appeal Tribunal (which was so busy that it had five parallel bodies hearing cases) or those for Middlesex or which-ever of the other nearby counties the man lived or worked in. The final rung was a Central Tribunal in Westminster, which largely heard test cases and relayed their decisions to local tribunals to guide work on future cases.

Derby recruits at White City.

Vast numbers of men appealed at the tribunals, or were appealed for by their employers. Roughly the same number (750,000) appealed in the first half of 1916 as joined the army in that period. Edward Robinson from Willesden attested under the Derby Scheme and successfully appealed to be exempted from conscription in early 1916, as his job as a baker was important to the community. By May 1917, though, his exemption was reviewed by the Middlesex County Tribunal and he was ordered to be called up and given four weeks to arrange his affairs. In other cases, tribunals were able to dictate that men should take up certain types of work to retain

A Metropolitan policeman chats with former colleagues who have been called up into the army.

their exemptions. Precious-stone salesman Sidney M. Fay from Cricklewood had attested and gained exemption as an unfit married man essential to the business' survival. In early 1918, however, the Middlesex Tribunal gave him two weeks to find 'work of national importance'; he promptly did so at army contractors Messrs Waring & Gillow, which kept him from being conscripted. Some proactive tribunals (including East Ham) were able to force local businessmen to pool their resources, or to actually run the businesses of their competitors who had been conscripted.

By the end of March 1916, Ilford's tribunal had received 371 Derby scheme appeals (since January) and 37 Military Service appeals (since 2 March). The Military Representative had approved 130 of these appeals, 14 were withdrawn and 39 had not yet been decided. Of the 225 cases the tribunal heard, 61.5 per cent were given exemptions of some sort, the majority of them temporary (meaning that the man would have to seek a renewal); another 37 per cent had their appeals rejected (20.5 per cent of all appeals received) and a small number of cases were at the Central Tribunal.

By the end of 1916, Chingford tribunal had received 354 appeals, of which 225 (70 per cent) were granted exemptions and 92 (25.5 per cent) were dismissed. Between 1916 and 1918, Croydon tribunal sat 258 times and heard 10,445 cases; Westminster City's local tribunal sat over 950 times and received 47,630 applications for exemption, over 70 per cent of which resulted in temporary exemptions from military service. Paddington tribunal, meanwhile, sat 102 times for 8,365 cases.

Those who appealed to them (especially when unsuccessful) saw the tribunals as merely stripping local communities of their young men. They were keen to find men if possible, particularly when they saw young 'shirkers' working in munitions factories nearby. Generally, though, the tribunals' job was more subtle than that. The mayor of East Ham articulated the dual role of the tribunal well in early 1917: 'As Mayor of the Borough and Chairman of the Tribunal, he was there in a dual capacity. To study the welfare of the borough was his first duty, but he had also, in the second place, to study the welfare of the country.' The tribunal's job was 'to weigh the merits and demerits of all applications that come before them, with a view to ascertaining whether the persons concerned could render more valuable service to the community by remaining in civilian life than by joining the Army.'

One group that received a large amount of attention was conscientious objectors – known as 'conchies'. These men were widely seen as shirkers, willing to let others die for the freedoms they enjoyed. Many tribunal members had been involved in local recruiting efforts and were not, by early 1916, in much of a mood to indulge the consciences of fit young men who rejected military service (those willing to do medical work were generally allowed to). Military Representatives could be particularly harsh, giving tribunals the rough, Colonel Blimp-ish image that emerges from the memoirs of objectors. Certain groups were given slightly softer treatment, such as Quakers, whose pacifist creed was well known, if not fully understood. Others who appealed on religious grounds often had belligerent Bible verses quoted at them and were asked what they would do if a ruthless German attacked their wife, sister or mother. Those whose objections were political – who tended to be more numerous in large cities like London than elsewhere – were greeted with incredulity, both by the tribunals and in the community.

The conchies are an important part of the history of Britain's First World War, an example of the intolerance of the wartime community to those who disagreed with the prevailing view. They were a small minority of appellants at tribunals, though: around 2 per cent nationwide, perhaps slightly more in urban areas like London. These cases largely came at the start of the process in 1916, as they were either exempted or forced into the army and did not come back to tribunals over and over again, like domestic or business cases often did. Conscience cases made up 1.7 per cent of appeals in Barking Town (19 cases, 15 of them in 1916), and around 3.6 per cent of cases in the much larger borough of East Ham (85 cases, 76 of them in 1916).

Among the 408 appealing at Ilford by late March 1916, twelve were conscientious objectors; all of them were given exemption from combatant service only, a common decision from tribunals early in 1916, under the (partially wilful) misapprehension that this was the only exemption allowed in conscience cases. For those with a strong objection to all military service, anything other than an absolute exemption was unacceptable. Even the non-combat option would mean being part of the military machine. Among those denied exemptions or who could not accept any military service, many either fled and became deserters from the armed forces or were arrested for their refusal to obey orders. The conchies continued to receive rough treatment whether in prison (for disobeying orders) or working in Home Office employment schemes.

During the war, more than 830,000 men enlisted in the army through the London recruiting district, around 17 per cent of the national total. London's contribution was slightly higher in the voluntary period: 18.5 per cent of all recruits before March 1916 were found in London, compared to 15.4 per cent thereafter.

Propaganda

Germany's armed forces and Kaiser Wilhelm arguably did as much as anyone to stoke pro-war and anti-German feeling in Britain; his description of his troops as 'Huns' (in 1900) and their killing of civilians certainly captured the British imagination. Public opinion was helped along by the establishment of propaganda organisations during the war. The Parliamentary Recruiting Committee, based at No. 12 Downing Street, urged men to enlist and used posters, speeches and leaflets towards that end, and a War Propaganda Bureau was established: it was usually known as Wellington House, after the building on Buckingham Gate in which it was based. Led by Liberal MP C.F.G. Masterman, its work was primarily aimed at an international (neutral) audience and a range of authors produced books and pamphlets espousing the British Government's position. One of the authors was novelist John Buchan, who later became director of the Department for Information when it was established in 1917; the following year, Lord Beaverbrook took over responsibility as Minister for Information, with Masterman and Buchan working for him.

Domestically, the combination of general public and press support for the war, German actions, and censorship of information that could be damaging meant that overt official propaganda was not really necessary early in the war. Local busybodies and thugs could be relied upon to interrupt pacifist meetings or German church services. Certain prominent individuals made particularly strong contributions to keeping up anti-German sentiment in London. The Church of England supported the war from the outset, but the Bishop of London (Arthur Winnington-Ingram) was especially notable for the vehemence of his anti-German language, casting the war as a 'great crusade' and telling audiences that killing any Germans – civilians or soldiers – was acceptable because the British cause was 'to save the world'.

The Bishop of London was a key pro-war propagandist, seen here preaching from the steps of St Paul's Cathedral.

Horatio Bottomley was perhaps the epitome of anti-German jingoism. Born in Bethnal Green in 1860, he came from a

poverty-stricken background to become an MP (briefly) and editor of the tub-thumping *John Bull* magazine. As the *Dictionary of National Biography* puts it, 'War afforded a national stage for his huckstering demagoguery. *John Bull* spewed out venomous chauvinism, demanding that all "Germ-Huns" in Britain, whether naturalized or no, be exterminated.' Bottomley addressed a vast number of recruiting rallies and patriotic (or anti-German) meetings. After being elected (again) as MP for Hackney South in 1918, he was unmasked as the swindler he really was and imprisoned on twenty-three counts of fraud.

Despite the predominance of pro-war and anti-German rhetoric, there was some concerted opposition to the war, and to conscription. The Independent Labour Party maintained a position of opposition, while the Union for Democratic Control argued for more open conduct of public affairs after the war. For their pacifist stances, both were denounced as traitors. A speech by Bertrand Russell at the Ilford Men's Meeting (a non-conformist group) sparked a lengthy and heated debate in the local press, with Russell and the Meeting denounced as unpatriotic. Sylvia Pankhurst later wrote of an anti-conscription meeting on National Registration Day in August 1915, attended by 1,000 people. Another rally in March 1916 saw Pankhurst and others speaking from the pedestal of Nelson's Column before ochre was thrown at her (and hit a 12-year-old girl nearby) as the rally was broken up by colonial soldiers and the speakers were taken away by the police. A Non-Conscription Fellowship joined the ranks of pacifist movements in early 1916, arguing against conscription and offering assistance to conscientious objectors – and thus facing predictable attacks for being 'unpatriotic' and 'pro-German'. Through the later years of the war, mobs could be relied upon to heckle their speakers or to break up anti-war meetings.

By 1917, the government were concerned about the effect of growing pacifist sentiment in the country and launched a National War Aims Committee (NWAC). In many ways a successor to the PRC, it was nationally funded but its meetings were largely organised by local committees. Across the capital and the country, meetings were held in halls or, more often, on street corners that people would pass on their way home from work. The speakers (normally two at each event, plus a local chairman) sought to reassure the crowd that Britain was fighting a righteous war, which they would win and bring about a better world. On the whole the speakers were well received; when pacifist arguments were aired in the crowd, they were usually argued down from the platform or shouted down by the crowd: the rain was frequently more of a blight on the meetings than were opposition voices.

3

WORK OF WAR

War and London Labour

'What haunted me was the plight of the people of Hoxton. It was a constant nightmare to us. Perhaps we imagined the distress which we felt would arise to be much worse than it actually will be. That remains to be seen. It is beginning to be pretty bad now.' When local MP Christopher Addison wrote these words at the end of August 1914, unemployment in the capital was just rising to its peak, bringing some of the hardship he feared, but not to the extent he and others expected.

Women working at the South Metropolitan Gas Works.

Tea time in the canteen of a munitions factory.

Autumn 1914 was the worst period for employment in wartime London. By November, Addison was noting the low levels of unemployment locally, helped by the employment of cabinet-makers (who had been hit hard by the outbreak of war) now making huts for the military. The peak of unemployment (among insured workers) was 10 per cent in September, in October the figure was 8.2 per cent and by December, unemployment was lower than it had been before the war; by April 1915 it was below 2 per cent.

Enlistment in the armed forces could be an economic decision, whether in response to unemployment or when employers laid men off to force them to enlist. By December 1914, enlistments had offset the decline in male industrial employment: the proportion enlisting was greater than the loss of work due to the war, so there were more jobs for those men who remained than there had been in July. There was no similar factor mitigating the contraction in women's work, though. For men and women, the impact was greater in London than nationally, although the authors of the Board of Trade's 'state of employment' reports noted that the London level of enlistment was higher than their estimate because the large number of enlistments from the commercial sector did not figure in the statistics.

Percentage contraction of industrial employment and enlistment in London, 1914–15 (from July 1914 level)

Policewomen going out on patrol.

	Men				Women	
	Contraction in employment	Proportion enlisted	Net impact in London	*UK average net impact*	Contraction in employment	*UK average net impact*
September	-14.0	8.5	-5.5	*-1.4*		
October	-13.7	10.3	-3.4	*-0.1*	-7.0	*-6.2*
December	-11.5	13.0	+1.5	*+2.7*		
February	-14.5	15.0	+0.5	*+3.6*	-3.1	*-1.5*

(Board of Trade 'State of Employment' reports, 1914–15)

The impact of the war on employment varied drastically, dependent primarily on whether an industry was important for the war effort, how it was affected by the disruption of trade (particularly with Germany and Austria), and whether the employers were large or small firms. Larger firms were more likely to win

*Female lamplighters
in the West End.*

government contracts, giving them stability or growth, while smaller firms struggled. The October 1914 employment report shows that 4.7 per cent of employed workers at large firms in London were on 'short time' (i.e. working less than their normal hours), with 2.2 per cent working less than three-quarters time. In small firms, 9.3 per cent were on short time and 5.8 per cent on less than three-quarters time. Meanwhile, other businesses had more than enough work: 4.8 per cent of employees in large firms and 1.4 per cent in small firms were working overtime.

*Fluctuation in male industrial employment in London,
July 1914 – April 1915*

Trade Group	Estimated number employed July 1914	Expansion (+) or contraction (-) by April 1915	Percentage of July 1914 employees enlisted	Net impact in sector
Metalwork	27,800	-9	17	+8
Machines and instruments	98,300	-9	17	+8
Chemicals	17,600	-7	18	+11
Clothing	67,100	-13	14	+1
Leather	18,200	+2	17	+19
Paper	8,400	-19	19	0
Printing	61,300	-16	14	-2
Wood	51,300	-21	17	-5
Food and drink	41,700	-10	18	+8
Building	117,000	-15	14	-1
Laundries	5,100	-14	30	+15
Total	*513,800*	*-13*	*16*	*+3*

(Source: Winter et al, *Capital Cities at War*, Vol. 1, Table 5.9)

Fluctuation in female industrial employment in London,
July 1914 – April 1915

Trade Group	Estimated number employed July 1914	Expansion (+) or contraction (-) by April 1915
Metalwork	7,700	+12
Machines and instruments	7,500	+10
Chemicals	6,500	+4
Clothing	153,300	-5
Leather	12,000	-21
Paper	18,300	-9
Printing	17,800	-5
Wood	7,500	+2
Food and drink	20,000	0
Laundries	36,500	-13
Total	*287,100*	*-4*

(Source: Winter et al, *Capital Cities at War*, Vol. 1, Table 5.8)

Among female workers there was a shift from clothing, leatherworking, paper and printing to metalwork and machine work, but an overall decline by April 1915.

Some of nearly 100 female porters at Liverpool Street in early 1917.

By the middle of that year, it was clear that more women were needed in the workforce and wanted to join it. A Women's War Work March was orchestrated by suffrage campaigner Emmeline Pankhurst and (less publicly) Chancellor of the Exchequer, David Lloyd George. Hundreds of women marched the streets of Central London to demonstrate their desire to join the war effort.

They soon got the chance. The enormous expansion of military production and the administration of the war effort provided a large number of jobs for women. Later marches demonstrated the extent of women's participation in the war effort. The number of women employed at the ordnance factories at Woolwich leapt up from 350 in July 1915 to 19,360 a year later: over a quarter of the entire workforce. As the table opposite shows, by July 1918 over a third of the workers at

Mrs Pankhurst at the Women's War Work parade in 1915.

Woolwich were women, along with nearly half of those at the Royal Gunpowder Factory at Waltham Abbey and 15 per cent at the Royal Small Arms Factory in Enfield.

Employment in War Office, Admiralty and Ministry of Munitions establishment (July figures, 1914–18)

	1914	1915	1916	1917	1918
Royal Ordnance Factories, Woolwich	10,770	45,570	68,990	72,410	65,610
per cent women	*0.09*	*0.77*	*28.06*	*33.05*	*36.64*
Royal Gunpowder Factory, Waltham Abbey	900	3,330	3,420	5,360	3,730
per cent women	*0.00*	*0.00*	*6.14*	*42.16*	*46.92*
Royal Small Arms Factory, Enfield	1,840	7,350	8,220	9,990	9,700
per cent women	*0.00*	*0.00*	*4.99*	*15.32*	*15.46*
Total	13,510	56,250	80,630	87,760	79,040
per cent women	*0.07*	*0.62*	*24.78*	*31.59*	*34.53*
Nationwide total	78,520	157,400	276,900	448,600	481,800
per cent women	*2.81*	*3.81*	*26.15*	*45.83*	*46.68*

(Source: *Official History of the Ministry of Munitions*, Vol. VI, part IV, pp. 61–62)

Those three sites were far from being the only places where men and women could work in the war effort. There was also the National (ammunition) Filling Factory at Hayes, Middlesex; Park Royal, a small arms factory in Willesden; Messrs Blake's filling station and Messrs Waring & Gillow (producing canvas products for the army) in Shepherd's Bush; the Anti-Gas Works on New Kent Road; Messrs Bell, Hill and Lucas (making gas masks) on Tower Bridge Road; Highgate Aircraft Factory; Messrs Dewhurst Ltd (which produced mortars and rifle grenades) in Fulham; Messrs Wilkinson's sword (and bayonet) factory in Acton; Brunner Mond's explosives factory in Silvertown, and many more besides. Some of these had been armaments makers before the war, but many had changed from peacetime production to munitions.

The largest war factories were broadly grouped around the River Lea (including Waltham Abbey and Enfield) and an area around Willesden, Acton, Ealing and Hayes, as well as Woolwich. The growth of Woolwich Arsenal meant that an additional 27,000 people moved to the borough during the war, putting pressure on housing and leading to the creation of new estates for war workers, including around Well Hall Road in Eltham.

Companies of all sizes, the government, and local authorities all took on large numbers of women during the war. The number of women employed increased, but more dramatic was the shift in what women did: domestic service had been the major employment for women in London before 1914, but by the end of the war women worked in offices, factories and in the streets across the capital.

Much remarked upon at the time was the increasing role of women in transport. The first female bus conductor began work in November 1915, on the Tilling's No. 37 bus, followed by more 'conductresses' for the bigger London General Omnibus Company

A female guard on the Metropolitan Railway.

from March 1916. When the new Maida Vale tube station opened in June 1915, all of the staff were women. At their peak level, women made up half of the 3,000 people working on the District line and a third of the Metropolitan line's 4,000 employees.

In early 1917, City clerk Joe Hollister from New Cross wrote to his father:

> [It is] extraordinary the amount of female labour employed in the City now, in the trains of a morning of ten passengers in a compartment there is generally an average of eight females, the Bank of England employ over 400. There was a flutter of excitement in Gracechurch St the other day at two girls with trouser overalls cleaning the windows of shops, the Railway Companys [*sic*] have employed them of course for a long while, tramcars, omnibuses, mail-vans, motorcars, Carter Paterson [haulage] vans, all the caterers, newsvendors, bootblacks, lamplighters, latherers in barbers shops, in fact almost every sphere of activity, when 'Tommy' comes home he will be keeping house and minding the kids while the missus earns the pieces.

A scene inside a cartridge-filling room at Woolwich Arsenal.

C.F.5. WOOLWICH ARSENAL.

In June 1918, another women's march took place to mark King George V and Queen Mary's silver wedding anniversary. The variety of roles and uniforms impressed the crowd, as American journalist M.V. Snyder wrote:

> There were between three and four thousand of them in line, representing all branches of endeavour. They were in working garb and made a colorful picture. The munition workers wore tunics and trousers of a cream shade while girls working in factories where cartridges and fuses are loaded wore similar costumes of red, emblematic of their dangerous calling. The land workers who do all sorts of farm labor were noticeable for their good looks and healthy appearance. Their garb is very smart, russet brown in color, with leggings, tight breeches and a smock that reaches not quite to the knee.

War altered the structure of the economy in London, affecting both male and female labour. By 1918, the number of men employed in government factories had increased more than tenfold; chemicals and metalworking had all increased by around 50 per cent, while printing and construction had declined by a quarter and a third respectively. The ease with which men could move into the war industries could be disruptive, as employees in other sectors could easily go off to munitions if they were unhappy with their pay or conditions. Similar flexibility in the war-production sector created a headache for employers and the government, which took steps to prevent skilled workers from moving jobs without permission: under the Munitions of War Act 1915, a 'leaving certificate' from their previous employer was needed for skilled employees to get a new job. Combined with the risk of being conscripted from 1916 if employers withdrew their exemptions, this gave a lot of control over where men worked. The system was seen as too authoritarian, though, and it was removed in late 1917.

The numbers of female civil servants increased markedly during the war – a fourfold increase in female employees, more than

making up for a 30 per cent drop in the number of men. In key departments in the war effort, women outnumbered men, by far in some cases. A large proportion of them were based in London.

Women took over a broad range of jobs in government departments; this group were messengers at the War Office.

Employees in key government departments, 1914 and 1918

	August 1914			Early 1918		
	Men	Women	Total	Men	Women	Total
Admiralty	1,632	698	2,330	4,063	4,101	8,164
War Office	1,445	156	1,601	4,932	9,665	14,597
Inland Revenue	9,030	250	9,280	4,618	4,549	9,167
Ministry of Munitions				6,756	9,925	16,681
Ministry of Information				124	236	360
Ministry of National Service HQ				298	770	1,068
War Trade Department				289	601	890
Ministry of Food				1,053	3,086	4,139

(Source: Parliamentary Paper, 'Civil staff employed by Government Departments', 1918)

DROP EVERY
MORTAL THING
& SEND
THEM
PLENTY
OF
MUNITIONS

*Munitions workers
in a Women's War
Procession, July 1916.*

The growth of the civil service, and particularly departments central to the war effort, had an impact on life in Central London more generally, as hotels, clubs and office blocks were taken over by government departments. By the end of 1916, Horse Guards Parade, Embankment Gardens, Whitehall Gardens, Regent's Park, the garden of No. 10 Downing Street, and even the lake in St James's Park, all held temporary buildings for government employees. Over 100 buildings were taken over completely or in part by government departments. Primarily these were in Central London, but the Inland Revenue took up properties across London, from Hackney to Ealing, while the Office of Works needed ten sites, ranging from Balham to Fetter Lane, to store supplies and the furniture removed from buildings occupied by other departments. Fifteen London hotels were occupied by government staff during the war, including the Hotel Cecil on the Strand, which became the headquarters of the Royal Air Force when it was formed in April 1918.

The National Portrait Gallery housed War Office staff. The nearby Eustace Miles restaurant served many of the clerks; Mrs Miles recalled:

It is most amusing to hear them talk of the Portraits that look down on them from the walls of the Portrait Gallery whilst they are at work. One girl always has Henry VIII in front of her, and she says she feels quite uncomfortable; for he stares at her so, and his eyes seem to follow her wherever she goes; so he doesn't seem to have *improved!*

Dangerous Work

War production roles could be extremely dangerous. Working with explosives in particular was inherently risky: the biggest industrial accident in the war was the explosion at the Brunner Mond factory at Silvertown, in London's docklands, in the evening of 19 January 1917. Michael MacDonagh saw the explosion from the south bank of the river at Blackfriars Bridge:

Women working for a baker in Forest Gate.

It was pitch dark … Then suddenly a golden glow lit up the eastern sky, making everything clear as day; and looking down the Thames I saw a high column of yellow flames rising, as I thought, from the river. This quickly died down, and the sky immediately became overspread with the loveliest colours – violet, indigo, blue, green, yellow, orange and red – which eddied and swirled from a chaotic mass into a settled and beautiful colour design. Dazzled and awestruck, I saw that London, so dark a few moments before, was made glorious as if by a marvellous sunset the like of which had never been seen before.

At first, people thought that it was an air raid, but word soon spread that it was an enormous industrial accident, the biggest in British history (although some still suspected sabotage). The explosion destroyed several streets of houses nearby; two oil tanks and two flour mills caught fire on the north bank and a gas holder on the South Bank was also set ablaze. An official report noted that most of the destruction was in a zone 220 yards wide, where all brick buildings were destroyed, while buildings within 500 yards were partially destroyed. Beyond that, the damage was mainly broken doors, window frames and ceilings. The explosion broke windows in houses in Blackheath and shops as far away as Brixton. Amazingly, given the scale of the damage, only sixty-nine were killed in the explosion; four more died of their injuries and another sixty-eight were seriously injured. Between 500 and 600 received slight injuries, most of these casualties being in nearby houses. Many people simply refused to believe that so few people could have been killed in such a large explosion; they also rightly questioned the wisdom of having such a large munitions factory in a densely packed residential area.

Silvertown was the biggest explosion, but accidents occurred in factories across the capital, including a major explosion at Hackney Wick TNT factory in April 1917. Hannah Spash from Belvedere was introduced to the king on one of his visits to a munitions factory in late 1917 and informed him of three occasions on which she had been blown up: one had dislocated her knee, another blew an arm off another woman, and the third killed two women. She told reporters that she went back to work because she wanted to help the men at the front, including her brother. In early 1918, Hannah Spash was awarded the Medal of the Order of the British Empire.

It was not only explosions that killed and injured. The chemicals involved in production in munitions factories in particular could be extremely toxic. Women filling shells were poisoned by TNT, which could lead to jaundice, turning their skin yellow and their hair ginger. The nickname 'canary girls' did little to help these women and the men they worked with; at least fifty-two munitions workers died of toxic jaundice nationwide in 1916 alone. The addition of doctors and preventative steps at munitions factories meant that the number of cases and fatalities fell significantly by 1918. Others suffered from sickness and serious skin complaints from toxic substances, while women doping the fabric skins of aeroplanes were liable to suffer from headaches and nausea. Laura Hoare and her children George and Alice Maud all worked at the Park Royal munitions factory. Alice Maud Hoare, who had previously worked as a ticket collector on the Tube, died in July 1918 from an illness contracted whilst working at Park Royal.

Strikes

One controversial aspect of civilian work in wartime was industrial action by workers. While service personnel were all too often risking their lives in the war effort, it was easy for critics to attack any strike as unpatriotic (and even pro-German). The strikes that did occur generally had little to do with the war effort directly and much more to do with the increasing cost of living and the failure of wages to meet it, just as in much peacetime industrial action. Following an increase in industrial unrest in 1917, the government ordered regional reports on its causes. The London and the south-east report identified the key causes, in order of importance, as: the cost of food (and the belief that profiteers were making money while working people struggled); industrial fatigue; inequality of sacrifice; uncertainty about the future; 'want of confidence in the Government', and other minor causes. 'Inequality of sacrifice' covered a number of elements, particularly around pay, but also in restrictions on movement of labour (under the Munitions Act, which was likened to 'industrial servitude'); distrust of the government largely concerned its treatment of working men, rather than the conduct of the war.

There were numerous strikes in Britain during the Great War, but far fewer than in the years before the conflict; fewer days were lost to strikes in fifty-two months of war than in the twelve strike-ridden months of 1912. The numbers of days lost to strikes was lower in London and the south-east than in other regions. There was a wave of strikes through the winter of 1917/18: in most cases, they were about pay and conditions and the workers very often won immediate concessions. This spate of strikes had died down by the time that the German Spring Offensive was launched in March, at which point strikes almost completely disappeared. More strikes then occurred in the second half of 1918, potentially in response to victory becoming

A trench-foot sufferer awaiting evacuation for treatment.

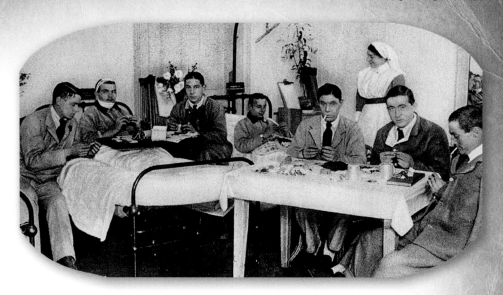

Wounded men in a hospital on Eaton Square, making cigarettes for their comrades.

an ever-closer prospect, with workers seeking to improve their share of the benefits. The new female workforce also undertook industrial action: in August 1918, female transport workers in London and across the country went out on strike for pay equality with their male colleagues. They received a war bonus, but not equal pay.

The most extraordinary strike in London ocurred on 30 August 1918, when the Metropolitan Police went on strike. The primary issues were pay, pensions and the right to form a union. The National Union of Police and Prison Officers was not officially recognised and the strike was triggered by the dismissal of a union organiser by the Met. Approximately 12,000 policemen went on strike; the government was shocked into action and gave way on all of the demands of the strikers, other than recognition of their union.

Medical Services

For all the new roles open to women during the war, many took on a traditional but vital female wartime role: nursing. There was a wide range of nursing organisations that women could join in the Great War, including the Army Nursing Service,

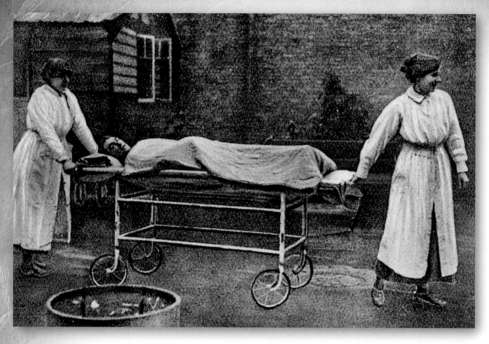

Transporting a patient at a London military hospital entirely run by women.

A different kind of battle: nurses and patients in a snowball fight in Southgate.

Queen Alexandra's Imperial Military Nursing Service, Queen Alexandra's Royal Naval Nursing Reserve, the Territorial Force Nursing Service and the Voluntary Aid Detachments (VAD), the latter jointly run by the Red Cross and the Order of St John. Nurses might be sent out to the various theatres of war, or work in the UK. Men also signed up for VAD and other medical roles, including the Royal Army Medical Corps and the Quaker-run Friends' Ambulance Units.

From around 7,000 before the war, the number of military hospital beds in the UK rose to 364,113 by the time of the Armistice. Of these, 36,664 were in London, slightly over 10 per cent. Five large 'General Hospitals' were made up of existing hospital buildings, other public buildings, new temporary huts and other local buildings. For example, the 2nd London General Hospital in Chelsea was made up of St Mark's training college, an LCC secondary school, and beds in four civil hospitals (Central London, Freemasons', Great Northern and St Andrew's).

London's General Hospitals, 1917

		Beds for	
	Location	Officers	Other ranks
1st	Camberwell	231	1,390
2nd	Chelsea	170	1,352
3rd	Wandsworth	897	1,503
4th	Denmark Hill	478	1,693
5th	Lambeth	62	600

(Source: *Official History of the Medical Services in the Great War*, Vol. 1, p. 74.)

Around 12,000 more beds were provided in fourteen hospitals housed in poor law buildings, infirmaries and workhouses. Five more hospitals were housed in pre-war hospital buildings, including the Maudsley in Denmark Hill and fever hospitals in Woolwich and Tooting.

Hospitals in Poor Law institutions, 1917

Designation (and location if different)	Beds for		Institution
	Officers	Other ranks	
Edmonton	0	1,810	Poor law infirmary
Richmond	0	514	Poor law institution
Southwark (in East Dulwich)	0	783	Poor law infirmary
Tooting	0	712	Poor law institution
Bermondsey	0	796	Poor law workhouse
Bethnal Green	0	729	Poor law infirmary (with beds in London Hospital)
City of London (in Lower Clapton)	14	713	Poor law infirmary
Endell Street	0	573	St Giles infirmary
Fulham (in Hammersmith)	0	1,130	Parish of Fulham infirmary
Hampstead	0	788	Mount Vernon hospital, Haverstock Hill hospital and New End poor law infirmary
Holborn (in Mitcham)	0	954	Poor law institution
Lewisham	24	838	Poor law institution
Mile End	0	864	Poor law institution
Military Orthopedic Hospital, Shepherd's Bush	30	1,070	Hammersmith infirmary and workhouse

(Source: *Official History of the Medical Services in the Great War*, Vol. 1, p. 81.)

Dozens of private hospitals, paid for by charities and individuals, housed more men, especially convalescents. Many wealthy individuals turned their London houses into hospitals and convalescent homes, particularly in the wealthy areas of Central and West London, where residents had rooms (or whole houses) to spare for recuperating patients. The 'Brassey Hospital' was set up by Lady Violet Brassey on Upper Grosvenor Street, while a Royal Flying Corps hospital was founded at No. 82 Eaton Square, Chelsea, and another hospital was set up a few doors along by the Countess of Dundonald. Other hospitals specifically served servicemen from the Dominions, including a hospital for Canadian officers at Hyde Park Place and the No. 1 Australian Auxiliary Hospital at Harefield House.

Wounded soldiers in the war hospital at the Coulter Hotel, Grosvenor Square, in 1916.

When the wounded arrived in London, they were collected from the train station by motor cars. Often – particularly early on – these were simply private cars lent by businesses and private citizens. Soon their reception became better organised, with the London Ambulance Column collecting the wounded, but this was still a voluntary organisation, with its vehicles supplied by private donors. In late 1914 and at times throughout the war, large crowds formed at the Central London stations to watch trainloads of wounded soldiers and sailors arriving.

Claire Tisdall worked on the Column throughout the war. Later in life, she recalled the arrival of the wounded:

And so I find myself back in one or other of London's stations in the dim light of the semi black-out. The air is heavy with smoke and soot from the old steam engines and fetid with the smell of stale poison gas and gangrenous wounds. I see again the long train with its Red Cross painted on the side: the sad procession of stretchers being carried with quiet efficiency by the bearers: the rows of waiting ambulances and cars. Sometimes, to add to the poignancy of the scene, there would be another gathering on a further platform. Young, tragically young and healthy men and boys waiting to embark for the Front. While here were the shattered bodies of those who only a few days ago were just as strong and vigorous.

Tisdall and her colleagues loaded the wounded, who ranged from those able to walk to the completely incapacitated, into their vehicles and drove them off to the London hospitals.

Nurses working at the hospitals often found it hard at first to cope with the cases they saw on the wards, such as young men blinded or maimed. Those who remained in their jobs, though, soon became hardened and simply sought to do all they could for their patients. It was a tough life for the nurses, many of whom had left homes elsewhere in the country to work in London. The Londoners among them could sleep at home when not on night shifts, but the others stayed in lodgings.

Vera Brittain worked at the 1st London General Hospital and described her routine there:

Not only men were mobilised; commercial vehicles were also taken on for war service.

We went on duty at 7.30 a.m., and came off at 8 p.m., our hours, including three hours' off-time and a weekly half day – all of which we gave up willingly enough whenever a convoy came in or the ward was full of unusually bad cases – thus amounted to a daily twelve and a half. We were never allowed to sit down in the wards, and our off-duty time was seldom allocated before the actual day. Night duty, from 8 p.m. to 8 a.m. over a period of two months, involved a twelve-hour stretch without off-time, though one night's break was usually allowed in the middle.

FROM THE BATTLEFIELD TO BLIGHTY

When a soldier was wounded or taken ill on the Western Front, there was a chain of medical posts along which he was passed until he could be adequately dealt with. The first was the regimental aid post, close to the front line, where the soldier could be attended by a Medical Officer and his orderlies. If the problem could not easily be addressed there, he would continue to a dressing station run by an RAMC Field Ambulance unit attached to their division. For serious cases, the next port of call was the Casualty Clearing Station (CCS), the first specific medical building at which patients were treated. After treatment there, the wounded could be transported on to base hospitals further behind the front line or back to the UK.

Hospitals behind the lines were not immune from danger, of course, and German shelling and aerial bombardment still threatened those being treated and those treating them. S.A. Gabriel from Streatham was gassed in August 1917 and sent to No. 47 CCS at Dozinghem in Belgium. On the night of 21 August, the CCS was bombed by German aeroplanes, with fifty patients injured and twelve killed, including Gabriel; a nurse was also wounded and four more were treated for shock.

In these attacks, the bravery of the nurses could be outstanding: in August 1916, Beatrice Allsop from Wandsworth and four other nurses were awarded Military Medals for their bravery when No. 33 CCS (near Bethune) was shelled by the Germans. Part of the building was destroyed and 200 panes of glass broken, but over 200 patients were moved to safety and two operations took place during the shelling. Nurse Allsop and her colleagues were among the first female winners of the Military Medal for bravery in the field.

Members of the LCC's Women's Ambulance Service identify the location of a call.

YMCA rooms and huts gave soldiers, sailors and airmen a place to read, write and relax, as seen here at Grosvenor Gardens.

Grosvenor Gardens. Y.M.C.A.

In 1918, another medical emergency struck the city as Spanish flu spread around the world. It hit London in two waves; one in July saw 700 Londoners die within a week, while the wave in the autumn killed 18,000. On top of the war's battles and air raids, the disease took yet more lives; so many that Woolwich undertakers called for soldiers to help them build coffins to keep up with the demand.

Khaki in the Streets

The wounded and nurses were not the only servicemen and women visible in the streets of London. Thousands were in the city on leave at any one time. Throughout the war, there were also periodic parades of men, women and machines. In the early years, these included units marching off to go to camps outside London, or to go to the front.

On 21 August 1914, Frank Hawkings of Queen Victoria's Rifles wrote in his diary:

> This morning there was a great bustle and excitement when the whole battalion paraded in Oxford Street in full marching order. At 8 a.m. we moved off, the band leading. By the time we reached Marble Arch my pack felt as though it weighed a ton, and I thought that I should not be able to go any further. However, we marched on through Kensington, Hammersmith, Barnes Common and Richmond Park. Eventually we arrived at the Star and Garter hotel where we now are. I must say I am much relieved to have arrived here. Any more of that marching and I should have been a grease spot.

Later on, there were the recruiting marches and marches of women workers, as recounted by MacDonagh and Snyder previously. Following the mass enlistments of 1914 and the raising of home-defence Volunteer Training Corps, London was full of uniforms by January 1915, as MacDonagh commented: 'Khaki is to be seen everywhere, and the voice of the drill-sergeant is to be heard from morning until night in the Royal parks, the gardens of the Inns of Court and in several of the squares'. Soldiers still guarded Buckingham Palace, albeit in khaki rather than the traditional red tunics, and when the king was escorted to the State Opening of Parliament in 1917 by troops from across the Empire, they wore khaki, as did he. There were also parades for the annual Lord Mayor's Show, which included captured German weapons, as well as soldiers and sailors.

Britain's new ally: Stars and Stripes alongside the Union Flag outside the Mansion House in April 1917.

When American troops reached London in August 1917 (the USA having entered the war that April), the city was decked out with the Stars and Stripes. Reporters were told to go easy on the American soldiers if these new recruits' marching skills left something to be desired, but if contemporary accounts are to be believed, they were in fact quite impressive. Michael MacDonagh wrote:

> The Americans are fine fellows physically – tall, slim, athletic, with long, clean-shaven faces. ... They marched loosely in fours, carrying their rifles at ease. Crowds lined the footways and cheered ... What an achievement

to bring them safely across the Atlantic, infested as it is with enemy submarines! And what a surprise to be told that only six weeks ago most of these soldierly young fellows were in civil life!

Many troops were permanently or temporarily based in and around the capital. London was already home to military bases, including Wellington, Chelsea and Hyde Park barracks in the centre, and Woolwich in the south-east. New bases were established during the war, too: Grove Park was home to the mechanised transport for the Army Service Corps; with 400 soldiers living in the barracks at the workhouse at its peak, over 287,500 passed through the base during the war. Dollis Hill was home to the Mechanical Warfare Supply Department, which experimented with new war machines. The mechanics, engineers and drivers there worked on developing new weapons, including the improved tanks used in 1917 and 1918, after the success of their first use on the Somme in 1916. Across London, soldiers and sailors also manned the city's anti-aircraft defences.

American troops parade through London's streets in August 1917.

London's Servicemen, 1918

In 1918, all British men over 21 years of age were given the right to vote, along with women over 30. Those serving in the armed forces (and aged at least 19) were also able to vote and marked absent voters.

Borough	Male voters	Servicemen absent	Percentage absent
Battersea	47,653	18,886	39.63
Bermondsey	29,352	11,790	40.17
Bethnal Green	26,844	11,734	43.71
Camberwell	74,171	28,854	38.90
Chelsea	13,432	5,413	40.30
City of London	24,694	3,145	12.74
Deptford	30,707	10,390	33.84
Finsbury	20,763	8,376	40.34
Fulham	44,283	17,988	40.62
Greenwich	27,079	10,070	37.19
Hackney	48,249	20,590	42.67
Hammersmith	31,932	12,285	38.47
Hampstead	18,153	6,656	36.67
Holborn	12,524	3,374	26.94
Islington	78,291	31,347	40.04
Kensington	36,910	13,867	37.57
Lambeth	80,602	29,339	36.40
Lewisham	48,111	17,572	36.52
Paddington	36,036	14,349	39.82
Poplar	41,698	14,929	35.80
Shoreditch	27,132	11,496	42.37
Southwark	46,612	18,280	39.22
St Marylebone	26,025	9,434	36.25
St Pancras	52,029	19,889	38.23
Stepney	44,697	16,669	37.29
Stoke Newington	11,904	4,894	41.11
Wandsworth	91,000	35,936	39.49
Westminster	37,300	12,255	32.86
Woolwich	43,339	13,762	31.75
London total	1,151,522	433,569	37.65

Among the parts of Greater London that were self-contained parliamentary seats, the percentage of absentees was similar.

Borough/area	Male voters	Servicemen absent	Percentage absent
Middlesex (whole county)	191,027	67,913	35.55
West Ham	77,276	29,686	38.42
East Ham	39,999	15,574	38.94
Ilford	23,818	8,110	34.05
Leyton	34,955	13,539	38.73
Walthamstow	35,086	12,852	36.63
Richmond	18,734	7,299	38.96
Bromley	22,853	9,347	40.90
Croydon	51,480	20,102	39.05
Edmonton	17,064	6,658	39.02
Wimbledon	20,745	8,299	40.00
Hornsey	24,555	8,390	34.17
Ealing	16,692	6,294	37.71
London outer ring total	533,037	199,379	37.40

Area	Male voters	Servicemen absent	Percentage absent
London county	1,151,522	433,569	37.65
Outer ring	533,037	199,379	37.40
Greater London total	1,684,559	632,948	37.57
UK total	12,913,166	3,896,763	30.18

These figures represent a snapshot of servicemen in mid-1918; it does not include those who had died or been demobilised from the military, and those who were conscripted in the last months of the war. From these figures we can estimate the numbers of men from London who served and were killed in the war (rounded to the nearest thousand).

	UK	County of London	Greater London
Absent servicemen 1918	3,897,000	434,000	633,000
Served during war (estimated for London)	6,147,000	685,000	998,000
War dead (estimated for London)	723,000	81,000	118,000

The Greater London figures may be a slight underestimate as it overlapped with other constituencies that are not included in the tables above, and because London provided more early-war recruits and so potentially more Londoners were killed or demobilised before 1918. Around 1 million serving and 120,000 killed seems a reasonable estimate.

(Voter statistics: Parliamentary Paper 'Return of number and class of electors, 1918'. Other statistics: Winter, *The Great War and the British People*)

4

NEWS FROM THE FRONT LINE

Londoners served in every branch of the armed forces and in every theatre of war. Around a million London men joined the army, navy and air force: others joined ambulance units and the merchant navy. Thousands of London women also joined the armed forces, or worked as nurses and drivers in the UK and close to the battlefields.

It is not possible to know precisely how many were killed and wounded, but some boroughs did keep a record: around 1,200 of Ilford's 30,000 servicemen died and 2,400 were wounded; 17,000 Walthamstow men served, of whom 1,500 died, 144 were posted missing and 373 were prisoners of war; Croydon's roll of honour lists 2,506 fallen and 207 returned prisoners of war. If the proportion of London's servicemen who died in the war is similar to that of the UK armed forces in general, around 120,000 of those 1 million Londoners in arms died during or immediately after the war.

Londoners at War

From the first encounter with the Germans at Mons in August 1914 to the moment the guns fell silent at 11 a.m. on 11 November 1918, Londoners were in the firing line on the Western Front. A million Londoners in arms means that around one in every seven servicemen in the British Empire's armed forces was a Londoner – including expatriates who joined the Canadian, Australian, New Zealand and South African forces.

A large number of those who left London to fight joined the London Regiment. Some first-line London Regiment battalions (those who had committed early on to serving overseas) arrived in France in late 1914. The London Scottish were the first Territorial unit to join the fighting in October 1914, but most of the regiment only served at the front from 1915 and some were sent to India on garrison duty, freeing up regular troops to serve on the battlefields. The London Regiment formed the infantry of four divisions: the 47th, 56th, 58th and 60th. Each held 20,000 men in three infantry brigades, plus artillery, engineer, machine gun, and other support units. Most of the men in the London divisions were Londoners, although as the war progressed units were moved in and out of divisions, including a set of Indian units joining

Large numbers of trainee pilots and their instructors were killed in accidents. In this one in Twickenham, the pilot was only slightly hurt.

The emblems of the four London Divisions

60TH DIVISION.   47TH DIVISION.   56TH DIVISION.   58TH DIVISION.

the 60th Division. Unlike other Territorial battalions, however, the London Regiment broadly maintained its regional identity.

The London Regiment was far from the only unit containing Londoners: they were spread across the rest of the army, Royal Navy and (from 1918) Royal Air Force. As we have already seen, there were London-based units in the Middlesex, Essex, East Surrey and West Kent Regiments and the Royal Artillery, while the Royal Fusiliers also had many London battalions. With such a range of service, the experiences of Londoners varied widely depending on where and when they served, and often simply whether they were lucky or not.

J.C. Mills from Vauxhall joined the Royal Navy in June 1915 and served in the armourer's crew on HMS *Pembroke* and later HMS *Vanguard*. He served at Jutland, but was killed in 1917 when the *Vanguard* was sunk by an internal explosion while anchored off the British coast at Scapa Flow.

J.T. Fullbrook from Camberwell was serving on the cruiser HMS *Venus* at the outbreak of war and remained with the ship through the conflict, patrolling the North Sea, the Irish Sea and the Atlantic, before going to China and East Africa.

J.A. Cranston from Battersea was a merchant seaman before the war and served through the conflict transporting much-needed supplies to the UK.

A London coffee stall proves popular behind the lines on the Western Front.

Also from Battersea was J. Hole, who was not fit enough to join the Royal Navy but was accepted in the merchant navy in early 1916. He served on HMT *Briton*, transporting troops to India, Malta, Egypt and Gibraltar, before being discharged as unfit in late 1917.

Most Londoners who served were soldiers. Len Smith from Walthamstow described and illustrated his war experience in the excellent book *Drawing Fire*; after enlisting in the 7th Londons in 1914, he fought and was wounded. He then worked as a sniper in no-man's land before being utilised for his artistic skills in a safer job, making camouflage and disguising gun positions.

C.F. Goode from Leytonstone joined the City of London Yeomanry in 1915, but was transferred to the 11th Royal Fusiliers before serving abroad; in twenty months' service in France, he was wounded twice: in the chest and in the foot. His neighbour, carpenter W.F. Harvey, attested in 1915 and was called up in August 1916 to work as a carpenter in the 17th Wagon Erecting Company of the Royal Engineers. Both men were demobilised in November 1919.

The army's officers were traditionally drawn from the upper and upper-middle classes: private school- or university-educated men who were considered natural leaders. Casualty rates among officers were extremely high and by 1918 more middle-class men (such as clerks) were commissioned as officers, joined by a smaller but growing number of working-class men. Lawyer E.W. Edwards from Blackheath was commissioned as an officer in January 1916 and sent to Ireland, where he served through the Easter Rising against British rule. He was later sent to the Western Front and died at Cambrai in November 1917.

Clement Attlee was a lecturer at the London School of Economics when he was commissioned in late 1914; he served in Gallipoli, before being wounded by a British shell in Mesopotamia and then wounded again in France. He ended the war as a major and became MP for Limehouse in 1922.

Regulations forbade non-white men from serving as officers, but a small number achieved it. Early in the war, G.E.K. Bemand simply stated that he was 'of pure European descent' despite being of mixed British and African-Caribbean heritage; his public-school background probably helped him to become an officer.

Footballer Walter Tull managed to overcome both the colour bar and the class bias of the system to rise from the ranks and become an officer in the Middlesex Regiment. Both Tull and Bemand were killed in action.

One of the many London expats who served in the Australian forces was F.P. Hewkley. Born in Stoke Newington, he emigrated after finishing school and joined the Australian Imperial Force in August 1914. He took part in the landing at Gallipoli in April 1915 and served as a signaller there until Allied troops were withdrawn at the end of the year. In 1916, Hewkley and his comrades were sent to the Western Front in time to take part in the Battle of the Somme. Hewkley was awarded the Military Medal for bravery after, in early September, showing 'great gallantry and devotion to duty in mending and laying telephone lines from POZIERES to Battalions [in the Division]. During the night 3rd and 4th […] he went out 4 times and mended breaks in telephone lines under very heavy fire.' The following June, he was wounded by a shell fragment on the first day of an attack on Zonnebeke Ridge. As he was being brought to a dressing station, he was hit by another shell and died eight hours later.

Jock Ashley joined the 7th Londons in 1914 and fought at the front in 1915. Of his experiences in May 1915, he later wrote: 'I have never seen from that day to this such mutilation of bodies by shellfire. There were bodies without arms or legs. It was our first real experience of anything like this and it didn't do to look about too much.' Late in 1916, Ashley was taken prisoner and remained in German hands until the Armistice.

Life could be tough for prisoners of war. Both sides on the Western Front forced other ranks' prisoners to do hard labour, often (illegally) close to the battlefield. Other prisoners worked far from the battlefields, on farms or in mines. The treatment of British prisoners of war was a great cause of civilians' concern and anger during the war. LCC employee E.B. Roberts was a prisoner of the Germans for three years and five months. After a few weeks digging up swedes and being fed a soup the men nicknamed 'Sandstorm' after its texture, he was sent to 'another camp where they were building Zeppelin sheds'.

Here we were treated in a most brutal manner [he wrote to the *LCC Gazette*], because we did not approve of the work, and were struck with sticks, but we kept to our word and put up with the treatment, and managed to be sent away after fourteen days as useless. Afterwards I got sent to a farm on a moor, which was fairly good, but did not last more than ten months. Again my luck changed for the worse, being now sent to a salt mine, roughly 1,800 feet deep. The heat was terrible, and the amount of work wanted was at times impossible.

A world away from those prisoners of war and the mud of Flanders was D.E.G. Quelch, who wrote to the *LCC Gazette* in late 1916 from his posting on Table Island, near Burma:

We are quite out of touch with everything outside as we get no news or mails except when a steamer calls with fresh supplies, every two months or so. Deer and other wild cattle are plentiful, also turtle, and fish of all sizes and colours. Unfortunately swimming is almost impossible owing to the large numbers of sharks. Cocoanuts [*sic*] and bananas are very plentiful.

Quite a contrast to his native Camberwell!

Many Londoners took to the air during the war, whether in defence of the capital, like J.E.R. Young who was killed in action trying to tackle the Gotha bombers over London, or over the battlefields. Most pilots were young, upper-middle-class men, like Young or P.J. Clayson, who shot down twenty-nine German aircraft in six months in 1918.

Not all pilots were officers, though: Flight Sergeant S.H. Quicke, from East Finchley, had joined as a private in 1915 and qualified as a pilot in late 1916. On 6 March 1917, Quicke and his observer were on an artillery-observation mission when they were attacked by two German fighter aircraft – one white and one red. Manfred von Richthofen, the 'Red Baron', was behind the controls of the red aeroplane, but on this occasion he only damaged the British aircraft. Two weeks later, Richthofen was out on patrol alone and managed to surprise an aeroplane 'spotting' for British artillery; he fired 500 shots at it and sent it tumbling to earth. When British troops got to the site, the pilot, S.H. Quicke, was already dead.

Women could not fight at the front, but they did serve in the military and in paramilitary units as drivers and nurses supporting the armed forces around the world. In her book *Within the Year After*, Betty Adler describes one of the women who served on the Western Front:

> There is Mary Bushby Stubbs, such a pretty, blue-eyed Irish girl, whose home is in London, and she drove the car to Louvain [in Belgium]. She had enlisted in the beginning of the war as a Red Cross Nursing Aid, but contracted a septic throat from nursing poisonous wounds – some of the wounded had gone for five days before they could reach the hospitals, she told me. Forbidden to nurse, she entered the Yeomanry motor car driving service and was sent to Chalons sur Marne in February, 1917. She drove an ambulance during the battle on the Chemin du Dames [*sic*].

Stubbs was awarded the Military Medal in 1918 for her bravery during an air raid, remaining with her patients as the bombs dropped, after the stretcher bearers had run for cover.

Some whole families served, in different ways: Philip and Emma Saul from Kilburn were in their early forties when the war began, but both played their part. Emma went to work at the Hayes Munition factory early in the war and later became a waitress in an aircraft factory canteen in Hendon; Philip joined the Royal Engineers in 1916 and worked painting iron bridges behind the British lines in France. Their daughter Rosina joined the Women's Royal Air Force in August 1918 and worked as a storewoman in London, first at Albany Street and later in Ruislip.

Four Colwell siblings from West Kensington are listed, along with thousands of other Londoners, in the *National Roll of the Great War*. John earned the Military Medal at Gallipoli, but was discharged from the army in 1916 with 'trench feet'; Frederick was wounded

Captured German mines on display.

GERMAN NAVAL MINE
TYPE
THIS IS THE LATEST TYPE OF
MINE THAT HAS BEEN FOUND
OFF OUR COASTS.
CHARGE 220LBS T.N.T.

Ambulance drivers in France – the tin helmet is a sign of how close they came to the battlefields.

at Loos in 1915 and died when his hospital ship, the *Anglia*, was sunk by a German mine in the English Channel; Daniel was taken prisoner in May 1915, escaped in 1916 and was recaptured but successfully escaped in 1918; and their sister Dorothy worked on aeroplane construction and later 'was employed in connection with life-saving devices at sea' until the Armistice.

For Valour: London's VCs

The Victoria Cross, established in 1856, was (and still is) the highest award for gallantry in the British armed forces. At least

The parents of Able Seaman W.C. Williams, after receiving his Victoria Cross from the King at Buckingham Palace.

Alfred Drake, from Stepney, was killed in action on 23 November 1915 and awarded a posthumous Victoria Cross for saving the life of his officer during a night patrol.

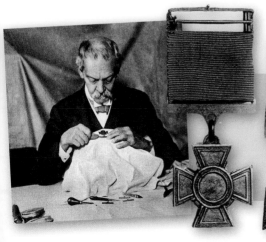

Engraving the hero's name on the reverse of a Victoria Cross. All Great War VCs were made by Hancock & Co. of London.

eighty VC winners had connections with London (see list on p.106), including a number of men in the Australian and Canadian armed forces.

These include Noel Mellish, the curate of St Paul's church in Deptford, who earned his VC between 27 and 29 March 1916, serving as chaplain to the 4th Royal Fusiliers at St Eloi. His 1962 obituary in *The Times* described how, 'On the first day of the battle, without any assistance, he brought in 10 wounded men, and on the second although the battalion to which he was attached had been relieved, he went back and rescued 12 more … His conduct resulted in the saving of many lives.' He was also awarded the Military Cross in 1918.

Charles William Train, a clerk from Finsbury Park, was a corporal in the London Scottish and served with the first battalion from the start of the war until he was wounded in 1915. He earned the VC near Jerusalem in December 1917, with the second battalion (2/14th Londons). Finding his company held up by a Turkish machine-gun crew, he crept unseen closer to the Turkish lines and fired a rifle-grenade from 60 yards that put most of the crew out of action; he followed this up with further grenades and rifle-fire, killing the Turkish commander, and then took on a second Turkish gun and drove its crew away.

Jack Cornwell VC.

A quarter of Great War VCs were awarded after the man had been killed, usually in the act for which he was honoured. The sight of parents and spouses collecting the medals awarded to fallen heroes was a poignant one for the audience at investitures. Gertrude Jarratt, with her daughter Joyce, met the king at Buckingham Palace on 21 July 1917, to receive the VC earned by her husband George. He had saved the lives of his comrades by standing on a grenade that landed in the dugout where they were

being held prisoner, shielding his comrades and sacrificing his own life. Another posthumous VC winner was Jack Cornwell, the 16-year-old seaman who stayed at his gun after being mortally wounded at the Battle of Jutland. After he was buried in a pauper's grave there was a public outcry, which resulted in a substantial sum being donated to his family by ordinary people across the country and a large military funeral for Cornwell being held in East Ham.

The funeral procession for Jack Cornwell VC, leaving East Ham Town Hall.

AWARDS AND HONOURS FOR LONDONERS

The Victoria Cross was unusual in being awarded to soldiers, sailors and airmen of all ranks, while other awards were rank-specific. Army officers could earn the Distinguished Service Order or the Military Cross, either for bravery or for good work; other ranks could be awarded the Distinguished Conduct Medal or the Military Medal, the latter specifically for bravery in action. There were also the Meritorious Service Medal, for good work, and the Albert Medal, for life-saving action when not under fire. In the Royal Navy, the Distinguished Service Cross (for officers) and Medal (for other ranks) was awarded for bravery. When the Royal Air Force was formed in 1918, new medals were created: the Distinguished Flying Cross (for officers) and Medal (for other ranks) for bravery in the face of the enemy, and the Air Force Cross and Medal for courage in other situations. A 'bar' was awarded for those occasions when someone earned the same medal on two separate occasions. In 1917, an Order of the British Empire was founded, with a range of medals and honours for military personnel and civilians.

There is no way of knowing exactly how many Londoners were given awards for gallantry or good work during the war. Among the 10,142 LCC employees who served, 733 were awarded decorations, including 68 Military Crosses (plus 7 bars and 1 second bar), 39 Distinguished Conduct Medals (2 bars) and 125 Military Medals (10 bars), plus 45 foreign decorations. If that figure is scaled up to the million Londoners who served, we can conservatively estimate that tens of thousands of Londoners earned medals for gallantry and good service. Soldiers in the 47th (2nd London) Division alone earned 2 Victoria Crosses, as well as at least 97 DSOs, 472 MCs, 321 DCMs, and 1,909 MMs.

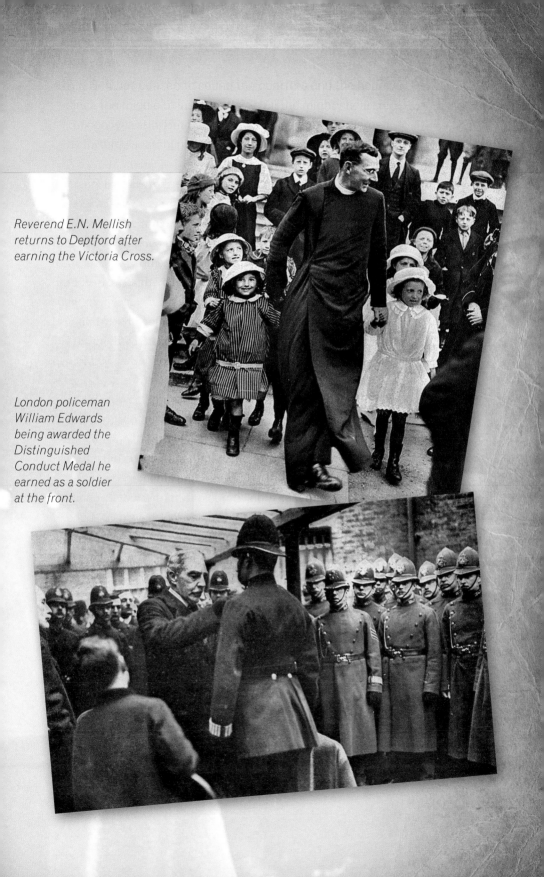

Reverend E.N. Mellish returns to Deptford after earning the Victoria Cross.

London policeman William Edwards being awarded the Distinguished Conduct Medal he earned as a soldier at the front.

Telling the War

One of the most common activities for British soldiers during the war was correspondence. Approximately 10 million letters per week were received by British soldiers in 1916 and at least 5 million sent home, suggesting that on average each soldier sent around three or four letters *every week*. Their letters varied from in-depth descriptions of places and events to brief reassurances that the writer was 'in the pink'. Many thousands of parcels were also sent, often including gifts of food (until shortages and rationing at home limited civilians' capacity to buy and send food).

The simplest form of communication was the Field Service Postcard, which gave the soldier a list of options to choose from: telling the recipient that he was well, ill or wounded, and whether he had received a letter or parcel. These could be sent quickly and easily, as they were not censored – any additional information added could be removed or prevent the card from getting through. The Field Service Postcard was used by soldiers too busy to write letters, giving people at home reassurance that the

Wounded British prisoners of war arrive in London, via Switzerland, in 1917.

sender was not dead or, if wounded, that he was still able to communicate. This effort was appreciated. Alf Page's mother wrote to him from Acton:

> I see by papers there has been some work near you[.] have you been taking part in any of it[?] if you do not feel like writing me a letter while you are so busy try and send a card just to let me know you are well[.] you know I am not much of a worry but still cannot help feeling anxious.

In their letters, servicemen were not allowed to talk about their location or give away any sensitive information about their unit, including the death or injury of particular comrades. As well as the fear of military secrets getting out, censors also wanted to avoid rumours upsetting families. It was still perfectly possible for false news to reach home, though: R.A. Savory, fighting in Gallipoli with the 14th Sikhs, was amused to hear that his parents in London had read of his death in the newspaper and received letters of condolence – they probably found it

British soldiers outside a ruined farmhouse behind the lines.

less amusing! Conversely, rumours might give false hope to civilians that their son, brother, husband or father was still alive, perhaps wounded or taken prisoner: Annie Bridger in Wandsworth wrote a hopeful letter to the War Office after hearing such a rumour of her husband Walter, who had died at Amman in Jordan in April 1918.

Ordinary soldiers' letters were censored by their officers. Once every couple of weeks, men were also allowed to send an 'uncensored' letter in a special green envelope. Men signed a promise that no sensitive information was included and a proportion of the letters were opened at base to check this, but the letter was not read in his unit. Avoiding censorship in the unit meant that men could write things that they did not want their officers to read. Officers' letters were subject to the same random checks as these 'green envelope' letters; the army's censors analysed these letters to gauge the morale of soldiers. Martin Hardie, a curator at the Victoria and Albert Museum who had joined the army in 1915, was one of those making these assessments, passing on the concerns and mood expressed in soldiers' letters to the high command.

A German aeroplane, paraded through London in the Lord Mayor's Show, November 1916.

A sentry on lookout on the Western Front.

Some servicemen wrote in-depth and often graphic descriptions of conditions and battles. Others wrote letters almost entirely devoted to their civilian lives: families, friends and businesses were constantly discussed. What civilians found out about the war at the front from these letters depended on what their correspondents wanted to say, whether they could articulate their experiences, and whether they felt the censor would let them describe what they had seen and done. Some men's letters could be little more detailed than the Field Service Postcard, simply a greeting, acknowledgement of any letters or parcels, and a reassurance that the man was still doing well or getting on fine.

Others were willing to relate the horrors of the front line. Eugene Crombie, a 20-year-old officer in the Gordon Highlanders, told his mother about the terrible conditions over the winter of 1916/17. Georgina Lee made a note of what Crombie had written, which focused on mud: 'added to wading through unknown depths of mud, there is the horrid sensation of treading on something soft and yielding which you know to be a corpse, or part of one, buried in the slush'. Still, he adds, even this is nothing to seeing 'corpses half-gnawed by rats'. R.A. Savory wrote vehement criticism of the generals and the newspaper reporting of the actions he had taken part in while in Gallipoli.

Even in the ranks, horrors could get past the censors: Jack Sweeney, writing to his future wife Ivy Williams in Walthamstow, let her know what he had seen and how he felt. In February 1916, he told her, 'We have been having a most horrible time, the War is worse than ever it was (War I said, I mean Murder) it is cruel. I am almost done'. That May, he described a British officer's body stuck on the German barbed wire and constantly shot at by the Germans in an attempt to hit any Tommies seeking to retrieve it. In 1917, as the Third Battle of Ypres floundered in the Flanders mud, Sweeney felt that he had to tell her 'what the Papers are forbidden to tell – the TRUTH': men dying in flooded trenches, freezing at night, wounded by shrapnel attempting to get along the Menin Road, and twelve men of his company killed and thirty wounded by two shells on the way to the trenches. To avoid censorship, graphic or critical letters were often (illegally) carried home by comrades going on leave and posted in the UK.

In addition to letters, home leave gave servicemen the opportunity to talk to friends and relatives. Many soldiers were unwilling to talk with their families about what they had seen. When Frank Abbis was awarded the Distinguished Conduct Medal in 1917, he refused to tell his family in London how he had earned the medal. After his death, his mother wrote to the War Office trying to find out: 'Although we have the Medal we do not know what he did to win it [...] All he would ever say was

I did my duty. That is all people ask. What did he do to win it[?] We cannot tell them.'

Some were willing to talk about what they had seen; many found it easier to talk to strangers, or people they knew less well, than to describe disturbing events to their relatives. In the restaurant she ran with her husband, Hallie Miles was visited by a former doorman who had been wounded in the jaw.

> In a quiet talk I had with him he described to me the awful moment when he was wounded. The worst part was that everyone thought he was dead, and though he tried to wave his hand, no one saw his poor hand. At last, in the darkness, he dragged himself by inches towards his trench – his jaw was hanging down to his chest – like a door without hinges. It is too horrible to describe all the sights he saw on his slow crawl back to the trench.

Civilians also heard details of the conflict from strangers when they sought information about missing friends and relatives. Some posted photos in the newspaper and talked to men's comrades on leave or in hospital. Beatrice Copping in Leyton

A despatch rider passing graves at Gallipoli.

The destruction of towns like Ypres was a common feature of wartime diaries and correspondence. By 1917, the historic Cloth Hall was in ruins.

was so horrified by the wounds she heard described that she hoped that the man in question was not her brother. Others asked the Red Cross to track down information about men who were missing; the 'searchers' (including E.M. Forster, who left London in 1914 to do this work in Egypt) often sent back first-hand descriptions, many of them graphic, of the events surrounding the man's death or disappearance.

Following the Course of the War

Londoners learned about the course of the war from a range of sources. Personal letters and visits formed one source. Newspapers were another; local papers published letters from men in the armed forces, as well as general war news items and lists of local casualties. National newspapers and magazines contained news of the war, with varying levels of belligerence, censorship and anti-German feeling. People also saw short news stories at the cinema. Rumours were a major source of 'information', many were completely false (like the Russian soldiers supposedly travelling through Britain to the Western Front in 1914) but they could also be the first inkling of a news story.

We have seen the impact that news of the fighting at Mons had when it reached the UK. From the start, people followed the course of the war closely, although once the trench lines had spread from the Alps to the Channel in late 1914, there was relatively little large-scale movement on the Western Front until the spring and summer of 1918. After the fighting of autumn 1914 and their horror at the German use of poison gas at Ypres in April 1915, British attention had focused on the invasion of the Gallipoli peninsula in Turkey. The first of several disastrous offensives by the British Empire's forces, it saw them and their French allies restricted to the tip of the peninsula and unable to shift the defending Turkish forces, who had reinforced their positions after an earlier British naval bombardment warned them of the attack. At the end of the year, the allies 'gloriously' withdrew from Turkish soil.

The first big British attack on the Western Front was at Loos on 25 September 1915; part of an Anglo-French offensive and the first time that the British had used poison gas in battle. The attack was a failure. Coverage and public opinion of the attack followed a pattern that later became familiar: initial reports told of great advances, but in the weeks and months that followed it became clear to everyone that it had not succeeded.

This pattern was repeated in the summer of 1916. Everyone knew that a big attack was coming: men on leave had told their families that something was up, some mentioned it in their letters; London's hospitals were prepared for large numbers of casualties. The first reports of the attack on the Somme on 1 July were positive. As the summer dragged on, more and

more names appeared in the casualty lists, more wounded men arrived in London, and the trench lines moved only a short distance after each fresh assault. People's faith in the offensive was bolstered by a new innovation in September, when the British used tanks in battle for the first time and made real progress, but the battle soon became bogged down in the autumn mud and petered out.

A month earlier, the British public were nonplussed by reports of a great naval battle in the North Sea – one that had actually happened this time, rather than the many that had been rumoured. Vera Brittain described 'a London seething with bewildered excitement over the Battle of Jutland. Were we celebrating a glorious naval victory or lamenting an ignominious defeat? We hardly knew; and each fresh edition of the newspapers obscured rather than illuminated this really quite important distinction.' It turned out that it had been a victory: although the Royal Navy lost more ships, the German High Seas fleet never again left its bases to threaten British shipping. Another startling event at sea, only a week later, was the death of Lord Kitchener after the ship taking him to Russia struck a mine, which was a great shock and became the subject of many rumours and conspiracy theories.

The failure of the 1916 Battle of the Somme to bring about the end of the war did not dampen the spirits in Britain as badly as might be expected with hindsight. At the start of 1917, there was optimism that, when the weather allowed it, the offensive would resume and the British would push through to victory. As at most points in the war, there was a feeling that it had to end in the next six to twelve months, although there was an ongoing joke that 'the first five years would be the hardest'. By early 1917, hopes of victory that year were high, despite the renewed German submarine campaign. The new war loan campaign was unofficially known as the 'Victory loan' and people openly talked about it as the 'year of victory'. In March, the Germans on the Somme withdrew to prepared defensive positions that the British called the 'Hindenburg Line', providing the British public with apparent evidence that the Allies were winning. In June, the British exploded nineteen mines under the German lines on

British troops on the Western Front near Zonnebeke.

the Messines Ridge and captured the ridge. The explosions were so loud that they could be heard in London.

Great hope was invested in the summer offensive of 1917, launched on 31 July around Ypres. Soon after the attack began, however, so too did the rain. The Flanders landscape turned into a quagmire through which the British Empire's troops pushed on with colossal loss of life and little territorial gain, finally capturing the village of Passchendaele, after which the three-month battle is now known. The failure of this offensive to end the war severely dented hopes that the war could be ended on the battlefield.

The most crushing setback on the Western Front, from the point of view of the British public, occurred at Cambrai in late 1917. When a British attack, including tanks, succeeded in penetrating the German front line at a depth of up to 4.5 miles, the nation rejoiced. Georgina Lee noted in her diary on 23 November, 'Today I had my Union Flag flying for the first time to celebrate this Cambrai victory … For the first time, too, since the war began, the bells of St Paul's and some other big churches rang a joyful carillon at midday, in honour of this first victory.' This celebration only made the reversal of the situation even harder to bear, as Michael MacDonagh noted on 12 December:

London lies to-day under a cloud of despondency. We are told that the advance of our troops on the Western Front, over which we were rejoicing the other day, has been turned by the enemy into a retreat. Most of the ground gained is lost; thousands of our men have been killed or maimed and thousands made prisoners.

Alongside food shortages and air raids at home, Russia's imminent withdrawal from the war, and failures by the Italian Army, this was crushing news indeed. The winter of 1917/18 was the lowest point for morale in Britain and in the BEF on the Western Front, alleviated only partially by the capture of Jerusalem by a force led by General Allenby and the ongoing arrival of American troops.

Early in 1918, a sense of resilience grew: the food situation was improving and Britons steeled themselves for the great German offensive that was almost universally expected. It came on 21 March and was portrayed to (and understood by) civilians as the crucial battle of the war, but one in which the German attack was being resisted. Just a look at the map told Britons how dangerous the German attack was, as land captured with great loss of life in 1916 and 1917 was suddenly lost (along with thousands of men and masses of equipment captured by the Germans). Field Marshal Sir Douglas Haig's order of the day on 11 April struck a chord with the British public, stressing the difficulties but reassuring them that they would win and that they were on the side of 'right'. It concluded:

> There is no other course open to us but to fight it out. Every position must be held to the last man: there must be no retirement. With our backs to the wall and believing in the justice of our cause each one of us must fight on to the end. The safety of our homes and the Freedom of mankind alike depend upon the conduct of each one of us at this critical moment.

Eventually, the German offensive was halted and the tide turned. By the summer, the British, French and Americans were advancing. Aptly (or ironically), one of the final actions by the BEF was in Mons, where their war had begun over four years earlier. By early November 1918, rumours were rife that the Germans were about to give in and sign an armistice.

Events on other fronts had less of a bearing on morale in Britain, although they were reported in the press. In 1914, British and imperial troops captured German territory in Asia and Africa (except in East Africa, where German General Paul von Lettow-Vorbeck kept the campaign alive until November 1918) and an Australian ship eventually sank the marauding German cruiser the *Emden*. There were also expeditionary forces in Salonika (also known as the Macedonian Front) and Mesopotamia (where the siege and loss of Kut El Amara in 1916 caused a brief stir in London), in addition to the campaign in Egypt and Palestine. British troops were sent to Italy in 1917, to assist their ally against the Austrians. In 1918–19, British troops also fought in the Russian Civil War in an attempt to defeat the Bolsheviks, who took control there in 1917.

Great War VC winners born in or connected to London

Name	Place
Edward Bamford	Highgate
Arthur Batten-Pooll	Knightsbridge
Richard Bell-Davies	Kensington
Frederick Booth	Upper Holloway
Rowland Bourke	Redcliffe Square
Cuthbert Bromley	Shepherd's Bush (also Seaford, Sussex)
Daniel Burges	Bloomsbury
William Burman	Stepney
John Campbell	London
Gordon Campbell	Croydon
Alfred Carpenter	Barnes
George Cartwright	Kensington
Bernard Cassidy	Canning Town/Fulham
George Cates	Wimbledon
Geoffrey Cather	Streatham Hill
John Christie	Edmonton
Brett Cloutman	North London/Muswell Hill
Clifford Coffin	Blackheath
Herbert Columbine	Penge
Thomas Colyer-Ferguson	Mayfair
Frederick Coppins	London (also Charing, Kent)
John (Jack) Cornwell	Leyton
Victor Crutchley	Lennox Gardens
Frank de Pass	Kensington
Donald Dean	Herne Hill
John Dimmer	Lambeth
George Dorrell	Paddington/Chelsea
Alfred Drake	Stepney/Mile End
George Drewry	Forest Gate
Geoffrey Drummond	St James' Place
John Dunville	Marylebone

Edward Dwyer	Fulham
Neville Elliott-Cooper	Lancaster Gate
George Evans	Kensington/Fulham
Humphrey Firman	Kensington
Arthur Fleming-Sandes	Tulse Hill
Edward Foster	Streatham/Tooting
Bernard Freyburg	Richmond
Cyril Frisby	New Barnet
Charles Garforth	Willesden Green
Benjamin Geary	Marylebone/Lambeth
John Vereker, Viscount Gort	Portman Square
Julian Gribble	Lennox Gardens
Reginald Haine	Wandsworth
Jack Harvey	Peckham
Alfred Herring	Tottenham
Dennis Hewitt	Mayfair
Frederick Hobson	London
Frederick Holmes	Bermondsey
George Jarratt	Kennington
Alan Jerrard	Lewisham
Frederick Johnson	Streatham
Richard Jones	Brockley
Henry Kenny	Woolwich
Leonard Keysor	Paddington
Cecil Kinross	Harefield
Arthur Lascelles	Streatham
John Lynn	Forest Hill
Arthur Martin-Leake	High Cross
Albert McKenzie	Bermondsey
Allastair McReady-Diarmid	Southgate
Edward Noel Mellish	Barnet
Harold Mugford	St James'/Bermondsey
Martin Nasmith	East Barnes
Frederick Palmer	Hammersmith
Frederick Parslow	Islington
John Pattison	Woolwich
George Pearkes	Watford
Charles Pope	Mile End
William Rhodes-Moorhouse	London

Frank Roberts	Highbury
Eric Robinson	Greenwich
Robert Edward Ryder	Harefield
John Sayer	Ilford/Islington
Cecil Sewell	Greenwich
Charles Spackman	Fulham
Robert Spall	Brentford/Ealing
Walter Stone	Blackheath
Frank Stubbs	Walworth
Charles Train	Finsbury Park
John Vallentin	Lambeth
Oliver Watson	Cavendish Square
Frank Wearne	Kensington
Ferdinand West	Paddington/Bayswater
William White	Mitcham
Geoffrey Woolley	Bethnal Green

(Source: UK Governments list of VC winners for centenary commemoration)

London's Buses at War

Nine hundred London buses were used to transport British troops during the war.

A familiar London sight in wartime khaki: a London General Omnibus Company bus on active service.

Almost unrecognisable, this bus saw action as the base for an anti-aircraft gun.

5

HOME FIRES BURNING

London in the Firing Line

Air raids were central to the experience of the Great War in London. For the first time in history, Londoners were attacked by the enemy from the air – first by Zeppelins and later by aeroplanes. These aerial attackers visited the city over thirty times; dropping hundreds of bombs, they killed scores of men, women and children, and injured hundreds more.

London was not the first place in England to be attacked by the Germans. After naval bombardments on the North Sea coast and air raids on East Anglia, the first Zeppelin appeared over the capital on the night of 31 May 1915. Almost a hundred bombs were dropped on Stoke Newington, Hoxton, Shoreditch, Whitechapel, Stepney and Leytonstone, killing seven (including four children), and injuring thirty-five.

After a raid on Leytonstone and nearby districts in August, the Zeppelins returned in force in September and October. Over successive nights in September, forty people were killed and over a hundred injured in raids on south-east London on the night of 7 September and Central London the following night. The 8 September attack caused the most damage of any Zeppelin raid, with bombs falling on a route from Bloomsbury to Liverpool Street. Eight people were killed on a bus near Liverpool Street Station and a single 660lb bomb blew out all the windows in Bartholomew's Close, but luckily did not hit the nearby hospital or historic church.

In 1917, the police tested out different options for air-raid warnings, including whistles, sirens and rockets. One other idea was warnings on motorcars, driven by special constables.

The car could then also carry the 'all clear' notice.

As the raids increased in frequency and deadliness, Zeppelins became objects of terror, having been viewed with humour at first. Many people still stayed outside to watch the raids, rather than retreating to relative safety indoors. Outside, they were more likely to be injured by the falling shrapnel from British anti-aircraft fire than by the enemy bombs. After the raids, people from across London travelled to see the damage, marvelling at the destruction wrought while, in the streets, children collected shrapnel from anti-aircraft gunfire. Rumours spread of spies somehow guiding the Zeppelins with their lighted windows. Blackout orders were enforced with vigour and the streets became darker than ever, adding to the sense of peril.

The next raid on London (13 October) was the deadliest yet: forty-six people were killed and nearly a hundred injured. Among them were people taking refreshment during the interval at the Lyceum Theatre off the Strand; a bomb that fell outside the Old Bell pub next door killed seventeen people. The landlord, John Nicholas Petre, survived but the psychological impact was so great that it caused his suicide in 1932.

The Zeppelins returned in 1916, with two raids in April that caused a great deal of damage but only one injury in London. A raid on 24 August saw forty-four bombs dropped on the Isle of Dogs and south-east London, killing nine and injuring forty-five.

The night of 2 September was a particularly memorable one for Londoners. One woman told Mrs Peel:

Bomb damage caused to suburban homes by the 13 October 1915 Zeppelin raid.

Freakish effect of the raid on a suburban villa. The roof of the house was torn off intact, disclosing a small room, the walls of which were unaffected.

Where a bomb fell in the street of a London suburb, making a large hole, which was filled in, and destroying the doors and windows of ten houses.

Effect of a Zeppelin bomb on a well-known London thoroughfare. The wood paving was displaced as if a squad of navvies had been working.

Six houses wrecked by one bomb. Scene of devastation where a Zeppelin's infernal machine found a mark in the London district.

Wreckage caused by a bomb on the roof of a house. While the explosion shattered the roof, the house next door was comparatively undamaged.

Room in a London business man's office, which suffered indirectly, but none the less heavily, from the explosion of a bomb in the garden.

DAMAGE IN THE LONDON DISTRICT AFTER THE AIR RAID OF OCTOBER 13TH, 1915.

Never shall I forget ... hearing an odd chunkety, chunkety noise. It sounded as if a train with rusty wheels were travelling through the sky. I ran out on to the balcony and saw something which looked like a large silver cigar away to my left, and I realized that it was a Zeppelin. Almost immediately it burst into flames and the sky turned red. Then came the sound of cheering. It seemed as if the whole of a rather far-away London was cheering, and almost unconsciously I began to cry 'Hooray! hooray!' too. But suddenly I stopped. We were cheering whilst men who were after all very bravely doing what they thought it their duty to do were being burned to death.

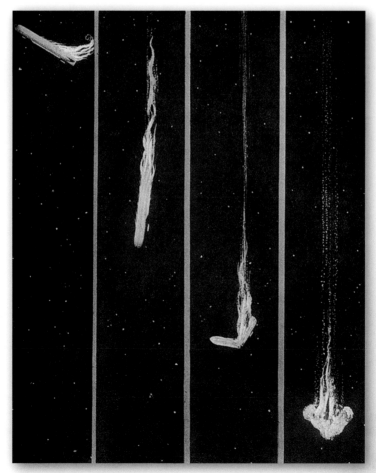

An artist's impression of the demise of Zeppelin L31 at Potters Bar, October 1916.

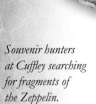

For Michael MacDonagh, seeing a Zeppelin brought down was 'probably the most appalling spectacle associated with the War which London is likely to provide'. For others, the sight of the 'babykillers' being destroyed was simply a matter for celebration. The crash site in Cuffley, Hertfordshire, was flooded by day-trippers wanting to see the wreckage and take home mementos of the first Zeppelin to be brought down over Britain.

Within weeks, another two Zeppelins had been brought down in two more raids. Following these losses, the Zeppelin campaign petered out over the winter of 1916/17. Soon, a more terrifying enemy took its place: Gotha and 'Giant' bomber aeroplanes. After initial visits in November 1916 and May 1917, their attacks began in earnest on 13 June. Hallie Miles wrote of the raid, 'They came over in such perfect formation that everyone thought they were ours. The Zeppelin Raids at night were bad enough, but these

Souvenir hunters at Cuffley searching for fragments of the Zeppelin.

The funeral procession of children killed in the North Street School, Poplar.

day-light raids are even worse, when the streets and houses and shops are full of busy people; the deaths and mutilations have been too dreadful.' During ninety minutes over London, these unexpected raiders killed 162 people and injured 432, including sixteen children killed in their school in North Street, Poplar. Two more children died of their wounds and another thirty were seriously hurt. The raiders had confirmed themselves as heirs to the 'babykiller' mantle of the Zeppelins, the sinkers of the *Lusitania*, and the German army in Belgium.

The horror of being bombed in broad daylight was soon replaced by the even greater terror of German aeroplanes marauding unseen at night. Where the moon had been people's saviour in the age of the Zeppelin, promising raid-free nights (shows were advertised as being on 'moony nights'), it was now a light guiding the bombers around the capital. Aeroplanes could stalk unseen across the capital, as Michael MacDonagh told an acquaintance:

The wreckage of the Zeppelin destroyed at Cuffley, Hertfordshire, on 3 September 1916.

> ... the terror of these raids is that you never can tell where the bombs will fall. London is too far-spreading for any part of it to be made invulnerable to attack. The aeroplanes also differ for the worse from the Zeppelins. We used to be able to keep the Zeppelin in sight in its course across London, but as for the invisible aeroplane you can never be sure where one may not be.

From 24 September to 2 October 1917, there were five night-time raids on the capital. The casualties were not severe, but the fear they created was. People sheltered, terrified, wondering where the raiders were. The noise of the anti-aircraft guns did not necessarily help – should it reassure civilians that the raiders were being driven away, or frighten them that the raiders were nearby?

Thousands of Londoners sought refuge underground in basements, church crypts and – in large numbers – in Tube stations. Up to 300,000 people sheltered in seventy-six Tube stations during raids in 1917–18, as many as 12,000 at Finsbury and Stockwell, 9,000 at King's Cross. According to housewife Lillie Scales, 'The tubes have been crowded with people, mostly aliens, who have gone in about 5 o'clock and encamped for the night, taking cushions etc. with them. It became impossible for travellers to get in or out of trains, and there was danger of people getting pushed onto the line, and also of serious infection.' That those sheltering were foreigners – and probably Jewish – was a common comment, probably due to many being poorer Londoners from the East End, escaping their less-sturdy houses in areas over which the raiders travelled to get to Central London. When families started going into the stations early on moonlit nights, more xenophobic observers claimed that 'alien' East Enders had been warned by the Germans that a raid would take place.

Michael MacDonagh rejected the idea that the shelterers were foreign but was one of those who could not exit the station because of the mass of people at Elephant & Castle during a raid in January 1918.

Whole families were there – mothers with babies and kiddies wrapped in blankets, sitting and lying everywhere, many of them happily asleep. Not a trace of fear did I notice – not the slightest sign of that nervous tension which is the common feeling of people sheltering in their own homes listening perforce to the guns.

After a raid, people emerged back into the streets, as C.R. Enock wrote in October 1917:

All clear! A car dashes past sounding the notes of a bugle; the streets as if by magic became alive with people whose footsteps resound on the pavement; up from the close warm tube-labyrinths pour the sleepy people; poor sleeping children, babies, tiny tots – poor little creatures; the searchlights 'wink' on the clouds, signalling that all is clear … Heaven has given us peace again.

People then had to make their way home if they had been out during the raid; trains, buses and trams were generally halted during air raids but services did not always resume after the 'all clear' if it was very late at night.

From early October to late January there were only two raids. On 28 January 1918, though, another horrifically effective bombing raid caught the public's attention, when the Odham's print works on Long Acre, Covent Garden, was hit. The building collapsed, killing thirty-eight of the 500 people who had taken shelter in the building's basement – the most casualties from a single bomb in London during the war. This was the start of another string of raids, with another the following night and three on consecutive nights from 16 to 19 February. The destruction caused by these raids included the residence of the Captain of Invalids at the Royal Hospital Chelsea, killing the captain, his wife, their two sons, and a niece.

Another raid on 7 March killed, among others, Lena Gilbert Ford, the American singer who co-wrote 'Keep the Home Fires Burning' with Ivor Novello. Journalist M.V. Snyder was in a theatre when that raid began:

Coming out into the darkness, one's eyes instinctively sought the sky. The sight was almost worthwhile braving the dangers of the raid. The heavens were criss-crossed with great pencils of light streaming upward from the searchlights located in the London suburbs and in the city itself. I started counting them and had reached more than twenty, when the rays from the lights in the southern part of the metropolis, which had been sweeping the sky, hesitated then all centred on one spot … This spot appeared to me to be just over Leicester Square through which I was then walking. Simultaneously, the barrage broke loose; it was very heavy, indicating that the guns were quite near. The other searchlights promptly focussed on the same spot then, while the first held the original area under surveillance, they methodically swept the sky surrounding it. The spectacle was a beautiful one, the long rays of light traversing the heavens, searching for the elusive Huns. Several heavy reports indicated bombs had dropped, but they were some distance away.

After a final deadly visit in mid-May, the German air raids against London ceased. By then, the capital was defended by 469 anti-aircraft guns and a balloon barrage, and the sky scoured by 622 searchlights, quite an advance on the three 3-inch guns set up as an initial defence of Central London in 1914. Londoners did not know that the threat was now gone, however; they remained on their guard for more hostile visitors. The sirens and gunfire that greeted the Armistice were initially mistaken by many for the start of another raid.

Searchlights were set up in 1914, including a very visible set on the arch at Hyde Park Corner.

Food

The war had a big impact on what Londoners ate and how they got their food, and food had a big impact on Londoners' morale. The declaration of war in 1914 prompted many who could afford it to hoard food, making it harder for those who could not afford to bulk-buy to feed their families. Lillie Scales recalled: 'August 4th. I went down to the grocer's and ordered in about £30 of provisions. A day or two afterwards the papers protested about this being done and said it was unpatriotic.'

Although hoarding died out as an immediate concern, shortages of food and increases in prices recurred throughout the war. In part this was caused by loss of imports due to shipping being used for war purposes, but Germany's attempts to starve the British Isles with a submarine blockade (particularly from February 1917) had a significant impact. Sugar, butter and fresh meat were particular problems and their prices rose dramatically. In response, some retailers instituted a system of 'linked sales', meaning that certain items could only be bought alongside others (e.g. sugar with tea), another development that favoured the wealthy over poorer customers.

There were attempts to educate people in food economy in the home, often seen as insulting by working-class women for whom the exercise of economy was not new to wartime. Middle-class Britons were urged to eat less bread, so that prices and scarcity

The flowerbeds outside Buckingham Palace used for growing potatoes.

would not have such an impact on poorer citizens, in whose diets bread played a larger role.

Rising food prices were the main cause for concern during the first few years of the war: in August 1916, the National Union of Railwaymen organised a large rally in Hyde Park about the high price of food. An official report on industrial unrest in London and south-east England in early 1917 concluded that the major cause was the price of food and the perception of profiteering. Shortages and poor distribution of food supplies were also major problems. For example, in April, *The Times* reported queues in London for coal, bread and potatoes.

Public or 'national' kitchens were opened from May 1917, allowing people to buy a full cheap hot meal to eat there or take away. Sylvia Pankhurst and her fellow women's suffrage campaigners had opened similar kitchens in poor districts early in the war, but they did not catch on until 1917, when Queen Mary opened the first national kitchen on Westminster Bridge Street. By August 1918, there were 600 national kitchens across the country.

As meat became more expensive and scarcer, people increasingly began to have meat-free days. Vegetarianism was a niche diet before the war, but there was now a flood of books and instruction on how to feed a family without meat. As proprietors of the Eustace Miles vegetarian restaurant, Mrs Miles and her husband were in great demand; meanwhile, Constance Peel had produced a vegetarian cookbook in 1907 and now published one called *The Eat-Less-Meat Book: War Ration Housekeeping*.

Across the country, unused land and open grassland was turned over to allotments to grow food for the home front in accordance with DORA, which allowed land to be claimed by the government and used for allotments. In London, vacant plots set aside for building work were used, as non-war-related building had virtually ceased. Tooting Council arranged for 12 acres of its land to be used for cultivation; Hendon and Bermondsey Councils allowed their parks to be used; Dulwich College set aside 11 acres for Dulwich and Camberwell residents to grow food, and the Bishop of London allowed allotments on his land at Fulham Palace. Elsewhere, the land around railway lines was taken over as allotments. The LCC had to balance the use of public parks for recreation and for the cultivation of food. Allotments were also dug in the Royal Parks (including a 'model allotment' in Kensington Gardens) and the flowerbeds around the Victoria Memorial became potato beds. By June 1917, the President of the Board of Agriculture was praising the allotment-growers of London, claiming that over 1,000 additional acres were being cultivated in Middlesex; Southall had 2,000 allotments and Wandsworth 1,200 (the latter up from 100 before the war). By September, 4,491 people were cultivating those Wandsworth allotments (314 acres in total), with another 362 on the waiting list. Early in 1918, mudflats at Millwall were turned into allotments, and extensions were granted to the allotments in Battersea and Clapham Parks and Shepherd's Bush Green, after which the LCC decided that enough land had been lost from its parks and no more would be turned over to cultivation. By this time, 1,600 of the 4,130 acres of the LCC's parks was being used for allotments, a total of 13,000 allotments (with a waiting list of 1,400). By December 1918, there were around 1.8 million allotments in England and Wales, compared with 500,000 before the war.

A German Eindekker aeroplane on display outside County Hall for the National Welfare and Economy Exhibition.

The problems of food queues came to a head during the winter of 1917/18, just as the loss of Russia as an ally and failure at Cambrai brought Britons' faith in victory to its lowest point. On 10 December, *The Times* listed the products in short supply: sugar, tea, butter, margarine, lard, dripping, milk, bacon, pork, condensed milk, rice, currants, raisins, spirits and Australian wines. Shops were smashed and looted in Leytonstone, Wembley and elsewhere. In January 1918, Edie Bennett in Walthamstow wrote to her husband in Mesopotamia that it had taken her over three hours to get meat: '... one dreads to open your eyes when morning comes to think you've got to line up all day for grub'. As well as meat being hard to obtain, butter had virtually disappeared and even margarine (once a despised substitute) was scarce: 'People who cannot or will not waste two or three hours waiting in frost, fog or rain have at present no hope of obtaining any supply of fat,' wrote one woman to the Bennetts' local paper that month.

'Multiple' (i.e. chain) stores were often the focus of the queues, as their supply chains made supplies more reliable than for other shops. One weekend in January 1918, over 1,000 people queued outside one such shop in New Bond Street for margarine and around 3,000 in Walworth, a third of the latter going away empty-handed. Wealthy suburban women were accused of exacerbating the queues by sending servants into the city if provisions were short in the suburbs, making it harder for working families to get their food. A queue at Ludgate Circus in late December included people who had come in from south of the river and from the suburbs in search of supplies. In mid-1917, a march of women from poorer districts in the East and North of London had converged in the fashionable West End to find sugar.

By the end of 1917, local councils' new Food Control Committees (FCCs) were able to tackle some of the problems of distribution, although not the supply of food. Where large queues formed outside certain shops, the FCC could intervene to send some of the supply to different shops, breaking one long queue into three or four shorter ones. On Christmas Eve,

Ration cards issued to Herbert William Wicks in Brixton Hill in 1918.

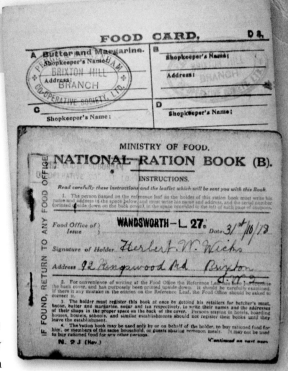

Camberwell FCC stepped in as margarine was delivered to one large shop; according to *The Times*, '3½ tons of margarine were commandeered and redistributed during the day, and it is claimed that in the afternoon there was not a queue in the area.' In January, the continued shortages and terrible weather drove those in the queues to angry protest: 100 women, turned away after queuing for margarine in Tottenham, marched on the headquarters of the local FCC. In Tooting, one shop refused to sell margarine to women who were not registered as customers there for sugar (which was rationed from January); a noisy protest was reportedly only kept calm by the intervention of the police and a change of policy by the shopkeeper. In the last weekend of January, an estimated 500,000 people were queuing for food across London.

A full rationing scheme, requiring people to provide a coupon to purchase meat, butter and margarine, came into force in London and the Home Counties on Monday, 25 February 1918, following local initiatives from shopkeepers and FCCs (including in Camberwell and Islington). People could only buy a certain amount of these products (and sugar), and even then only from the retailer with whom they were registered. Adults were allotted 1*s* 3*d* worth of fresh meat (plus 5*d* of 'un-butchered meat' like poultry or offal) and 4oz of butter. The introduction of rationing across the city dramatically reduced the queues, with

Edie Bennett remarking to her husband that 'this rationing has done away with the blessed lining up for hours, it's a treat to go out and walk along the pavement instead of the road'. Meat rationing spread to the rest of the country in April, and in July the system was expanded to include lard and bacon; although not rationed, people could only buy tea from their registered supplier. Under this scheme, 1s 9d worth of fresh meat, 8oz of bacon (or 12oz of ham), 8oz of sugar, 5oz of butter and 2oz of lard was the weekly adult ration. Rationing quelled the lines, ending a phenomenon that had given the English vocabulary a new word: 'queuing'.

What people ate changed in response to availability and prices. While consumption of bread, milk and tinned meat was stable, by 1918 butter was almost unknown and people were eating far more bacon and margarine. Britons did not starve, but it took the crisis of 1917–18 for the problem of distribution to be adequately addressed, restoring people's faith in the food supply.

Food prices (1914–16) and consumption (1914–18) in London

Foodstuff	Price (As percentage of July 1914 level)			Consumption 1918 (As percentage of 1913–14 level)
	October 1914	October 1915	November 1916	
Bread and flour	111	141	163	96
Milk	-	115	143	107
Butter	108	127	150	14
Margarine	123	113	122	215
Potatoes	93	96	169	145
Beef	109	149	169	Fresh meat: 47
Mutton	115	152	176	
Bacon	-	-	-	221
Tinned/frozen meat	-	-	-	96
Sugar	163	184	160	54
Cost of living	*110*	*132*	*160*	-

(Source: Winter et al, *Capital Cities at War*, Vol. 1, tables 11.5 and 11.6)

Home on Leave

London's railway termini were major waypoints for millions of service personnel during the war: every day, thousands passed through on their way home or returning to the front. Across the country, local men returned to their families for a few brief days away from army life and the dangers of the war. In addition to Londoners arriving home each day, those travelling to other parts of Britain passed through the city, while men and women who had travelled from across the Empire to serve in Europe often spent their 'home' leave in the imperial capital.

Men looked forward to this leave enormously. A British Army morale report in 1916 concluded that, 'The most frequent complaint … is in regard to leave; its infrequency and uneven distribution. It is no exaggeration to say that leave is the commonest topic of correspondence … The Army lives for leave.'

Hallie Miles watched the leave train arrive at Victoria Station in March 1915:

It was a very intense time, waiting for the wonderful train to come in with its heroic burden … [The] train seemed *more* than a train, as it slowly slipped into the siding. In one instant the doors all flew open, and strange objects poured out. They seemed almost to resemble Arctic explorers, or Esquimaux, than ordinary soldiers. Most of them had on sheepskin coats, strange fur caps and woollen [balaclava] helmets; and their khaki was black; some were in rags, and oh! the mud on their boots and legs. The colour of their faces was strange too, so weather-worn and weather-beaten. But the saddest part of all was the stern gravity of their expressions, as if the 'veil' had been lifted and they had seen things they could never speak of and never forget … They all looked *dreadfully* tired. It was the most wonderful and thrilling crowd I have ever seen. It made one realise what the War means more than anything else has ever done.

Servicemen made for an odd sight on the Tube, as Georgina Lee noted: 'A number of soldiers, just back for a few days' leave came into the train with all the dust and dirt of the trenches thick on their boots and accoutrements. It is so strange to think that in a few hours they are in our midst, fresh from the firing line.' Vera Brittain remembered that in 1915 it was fashionable for officers home on leave from the front to look as shabby as possible, to distinguish themselves from those still training; later, when most young officers had served abroad, the fashion died out.

Ordinary British servicemen serving on the Western Front were entitled to a few days at home every year; officers were able to go home more frequently. The length of this leave increased from three days early in the war to a week and finally to ten days by 1918. In mid-1917, 50,000 servicemen were on leave from the Western Front at any given point, roughly 2.5 per cent of the whole BEF. This increased to around 4 per cent (80,000) by the end of the year but fell to 2.2 per cent during the return to mobile warfare in mid-1918. From the perspective of communities at home, more service personnel were around since those based at home or recuperating from wounds or sickness were also able to get home on leave. Meanwhile, those based further away might not come back for years, if at all; Edie Bennett's husband served in Mesopotamia from 1917 to 1919 without any home leave. At the end of February 1918, there were 900 servicemen on leave in Walthamstow, roughly 7 per cent of the local men absent on war service.

Following appeals in the papers for something to be done to greet those arriving on leave, groups of ladies volunteered to run free buffets at London's termini. The first was set up at London Bridge in late 1914, followed in February and March 1915 by buffets at Victoria and Liverpool Street, and soon there were buffets at all of the major termini. These buffets supplied a hot drink and a meal to servicemen as they arrived in London or waited for their train back to the front. They were also useful for the London Ambulance Column volunteers, who could end up spending the whole day or night

General View, Eagle Hut, London.

A postcard of the YMCA 'Eagle Hut', sent home to New York by American sailor George Preece in 1919.

in stations or on the road. The buffet at Waterloo (located in a tunnel under the platforms) served meals and refreshments to 8 million service personnel; the Victoria buffet, meanwhile, served 12 million.

On home leave, Londoners and other Britons were able to rejoin their civilian lives, while those from the Empire and Dominions could see the sights of the capital and stay in the YMCAs and other hotels, where they could get tea, play billiards, read and sleep. YMCA huts were established close to the main train stations and around the city; the site of a planned Shakespeare theatre on Gower Street was used for one, named the 'Shakespeare Hut' (now the site of the London School of Hygiene and Tropical Medicine). On Aldwych, a YMCA hut was opened for Americans in August 1917, the 'Eagle Hut' serving 2 million meals in its two years of operation. Further up the Strand was the Canadian equivalent: the 'Beaver Hut'.

YMCA huts were very heavily used by servicemen on leave; George Preece wrote home in 1919 from the Eagle Hut that 'The YMCA men and women are wonderful and do everything

 3 A.M. IN A LONDON STATION HUT

possible for us'. Journalist C. Sheridan-Jones was critical, though: 'Tommy gets tired of the severe, not to say bleak, interior of these huts … He longs for warmth and colour, for a chat with pals, to whom he can talk freely and easily, for a little of that social relaxation that every son of Adam, who is not also a teetotaller, delights in.' With pubs shut most of the day, he claimed that men were tempted into less salubrious and unlicensed premises. The area around Waterloo was particularly known for the availability of prostitutes, whom the authorities sought to avoid soldiers visiting. The YMCA huts were popular nonetheless, both for relaxation and as somewhere to sleep. On 25 September 1918, *The Times* reported that over 13,500 soldiers and sailors had slept at various YMCA huts in London during the previous week: 2,640 at High Holborn, 2,247 at the Shakespeare Hut, 1,872 at Waterloo, 1,734 at London Bridge, 1,205 at Aldwych, 1,953 at the Eagle Hut, and 1,092 at the Beaver Hut.

A free newspaper was provided to servicemen on leave. *Welcome* contained patriotic propaganda and cartoons, as well as a map of London (showing the YMCA accommodation), transport information, warnings about dodgy tradesmen, and articles. As well as this service, a wooden hut was erected in Trafalgar Square for the express purpose of organising sightseeing trips for visiting service personnel. Large numbers of servicemen also went to the theatres and cinemas and special performances were put on for the wounded.

Back to the Front

In general, soldiers enjoyed their leave and regretted the need to go back. For most, it was a welcome relief from the strains of the war. Len Smith recalled 'a glorious week of joy and the right brand of excitement', despite being woken by Zeppelin raids. Others felt detached from the world they encountered back at home, so different from the everyday dangers of the front.

All too soon, they had to return to their units. Jock Ashley's home leave ended with a 'Pretty ghastly evening, everybody trying to look and be cheerful when they didn't feel like it – myself included. I suppose that last six days were the best I had ever spent.' Overstaying a leave allocation could mean punishment for themselves and possibly also a delay in their comrades' leaves – and one certainly would not want to get between a group of battle-hardened Tommies and their home leave!

The early departure of the train back to the front could mean a stay overnight in a YMCA or in the station itself. Ben Keeling arrived at Liverpool Street after leave in Essex in 1914 and hitched a lift to Victoria:

An extraordinary night. Row after row of England's fighting men lying sleeping on the platform or sitting on their packs reading the papers. I have just had a lovely 'kip' with my back against a corner, but the owner of a stall has come along and wakened me in order to open his shop front.

A YMCA tea room at Waterloo Road for wives accompanying men on their way back to the front.

Hallie Miles watched the 'good-bye' train one morning:

The men looked very brave, but their faces were very set … Soon the platform was crowded with this wonderful army of men and women who were fighting back the tears so bravely, and each helping the other by their own courage. Then came the moment when the first dreaded whistle sounded; it seemed more like a 'trumpet call' than the whistle of an ordinary engine. The very air became suddenly charged with intensest [*sic*] feeling. We all held our breaths; perfect silence reigned, for we knew the 'good-byes' were being said; we knew that for some the last kiss was being given. Then there was a banging of doors, and the last whistle sounded. The train slowly moved off, as if it could not *bear* to go, and the platform was left with only women, a few fathers, and some very depressed doggies. I never saw such a sight as it was when the khaki arms were waving out of the windows to those dear ones who were left standing on the platform as long as the train was in sight.

*Soldiers leaving
Victoria for the
front after leave
at home over
Christmas 1915.*

*Final preparations
being made for a
war-photograph
exhibition at
the Victoria and
Albert Museum.
The central image is
of Admiral Beatty.*

Len Smith's train 'steamed out of Victoria about 8 a.m. amid a storm of cheers and farewells from the very crowded platform. We looked a cheery lot of fellows till we'd travelled out of sight then everybody seemed to grow glum at the prospect of leaving it all again for goodness knew how long.'

The trains took them from London to the South Coast – usually Folkestone – for a crossing to Boulogne, from where they returned to their units to wait for their next leave, or for a Blighty wound they hoped would get them home without permanent disfigurement. Jock Ashley returned from leave in February 1916:

> Sleep the night in Boulogne. Very cold. I have rarely been so fed up in my life. … The mud everywhere was thick and the place black as pitch, everybody fed up to the teeth, it being forced upon us so strongly that we were in France again, amongst the mud – some difference from the London streets.

Entertainment

London had plenty of entertainments to offer in 1914: theatres, cinemas, sports, restaurants, museums, galleries, pubs and parks. The war had an impact on them all in different ways.

Theatre and cinema offered people an escape from the war. Although there were war-themed plays and films, and concerts to raise money for the war effort, most of what was on offer was the same as before the war: escapism and entertainment. Mrs Peel remembered, 'The theatres at this period produced little but the lightest plays and revues, and many protests were made by the more seriously minded regarding the suggestiveness and impropriety of certain stage productions and the scanty clothing worn by the girls employed.' London's most popular wartime play was of just this type: the Orientalist romp *Chu Chin Chow*, which ran from August 1916 to July 1921. Theatres were affected by the loss of many young men from their casts, but were still enormously popular. 'Managers have usually boasted of the number of pretty girls in their shows,' M.V. Snyder wrote in early 1918. 'If this war continues, it is possible press agents may be driven to lay stress on the number of able-bodied men.'

The 1916 film *The Battle of the Somme* was the biggest cinema hit of the war: its mixture of real and staged footage brought the battlefield to life vividly for civilians. Around 20 million Britons saw it in its first six weeks – roughly half of the civilian population. Attempts to repeat this success with later war films failed and the most popular types of movies during the war, as before it, were comedies (especially Charlie Chaplin) and weekly serials.

In early 1916, the government announced that a number of national museums and galleries in the capital would be closed in the name of efficiency. A horrified public response kept the National Gallery and the Victoria and Albert Museum open, but the National Portrait Gallery, the British Museum, the Science Museum, the Tate Gallery (now Tate Britain) and the Wallace Collection closed for the duration, many becoming government offices. The closure of the British Museum was seen as particularly inconvenient to servicemen from the Dominions, who might never have the chance to return to London.

The war significantly affected Britons' drinking habits, too. Not only was what people ate altered by the availability and cost of food, but regulations restricted what and when they could drink. From November 1915, pubs were only able to serve alcohol between noon and 2.30 p.m. and 6.30 and 9.30p.m., beer was watered down and 'treating' was banned – people could no longer buy drinks for each other.

In 1917, C. Sheridan-Jones complained about the 'puritan' restrictions on drinking and buying drinks for others. This had, he wrote, simply driven drinking underground, into unlicensed pubs and clubs that appeared and disappeared around Central London, where alcohol could be freely purchased, often alongside cocaine and opium:

London, from being a city of bright taverns and happy-go-lucky music halls, full of jollity, high spirits and fun, has become a darkened territory, with secret meeting-places and obscure flats where cocaine is sold and injected; where opium smoking is practiced, amid surroundings of Eastern magnificence; where men and women indulge in strange, exotic pleasures as alien to our race as the secrecy that covers them.

According to Mrs Peel:

The growth of the night club was an outstanding feature of war-time life. Such places had always existed, but it was not until after war was declared that they were patronised by women and young girls of good reputation. By the winter of 1915 it was reported that there were 150 night clubs in Soho alone, some of them of very doubtful character. Many complaints were made, but as fast as one club was forced to shut another opened.

This was not a mass black market, however: Sheridan-Jones wrote that 'not all London is underground. The great mass of people are untouched, unpoisoned.'

Some restaurants also allowed the better-off to escape the wartime puritanism and shortages: in November 1917 a *Herald* journalist published a description of the scandalously large and decadent meals offered at the Ritz, in contrast to the increasing difficulties ordinary people faced in feeding their families. In 1918, M.V. Snyder was 'surprised to find after dining at several of the best known restaurants that, beneath its pall, London still retains much of its characteristic night life. This is only the case, however, in the big hotels', such as the Ritz and the Savoy, where men and women still wore their evening finest and partied on until 11.30 p.m.

Professional sport died out during the first year of the war, although the association football season continued until May 1915, amidst general outcry about the professional players putting their pay packets ahead of their country. County cricket ceased a few weeks into the war, with games scheduled for September 1914 abandoned. Unlike their football counterparts, London's county cricket teams finished on a high; each won their final match and

Surrey topped the championship table, with Middlesex finishing second. Tottenham Hotspur and Chelsea, meanwhile, were the bottom two teams in football's First Division. Neither sport was completely killed off by the war, though; football leagues continued at a regional level while charity and inter-service cricket matches continued throughout the war.

London's parks were also changed by the war. Used for military parades and exercises early in the war, by 1916 much of the green space in Central London was being built on for temporary government offices: Regent's Park hosted a large sorting office for letters and parcels going to the front, for example. As noted previously, allotments also occupied public open spaces. People could still, however, enjoy the open spaces further out in the boroughs and suburbs, although they might find troops training, or a searchlight or anti-aircraft gun there.

Fundraising

A common sight on the streets of London, and across Britain, was charity donation collectors. They collected for existing charities like the YMCA and Red Cross and new war charities, including Belgian refugees and British prisoners of war.

The most prominent mode of collection was the 'flag day', when a charity flooded the streets with volunteers (usually young women) selling small paper flags to passers-by. The apparently constant stream of 'flag days' and appeals began to grate on many people – the *Ilford Recorder* published a grumbling poem in June 1916 called 'Too Many Flag Days'. When reports circulated that flag days were 'flagging' (in the obvious and overused pun), the *Barking Advertiser* disagreed: 'Flag days are not flagging. They seem, in fact, to increase in number in our midst, and scarcely a week goes by without the observance of some special "day".'

Flag days and charitable campaigns did decline in their prominence in the press in the second half of the war, but this does not seem to have affected their success. Historian Peter

Girls collecting money for the wounded at Caledonian Road flower market

Grant has shown that even as times became tougher, charitable giving increased in London, with 263 collections in 1916/17 raising £268,736 and 261 in 1918 raising £391,864 (an increase of a quarter, even taking inflation into account). Donations to the nationwide '*Times* Fund' also increased every year. These increases are all the more remarkable given the shift in emphasis in the press from charity campaigns to war savings and war bonds.

The public were urged to invest in war bonds or war loan certificates, which put their money into the war effort in exchange for a dividend after the war varying between 3.5 and 5 per cent. War savings associations were set up to enable people to invest in the war effort: there were 4,078 in London and 828 in Middlesex, of which over 2,000 were in businesses and 450 in munitions works, the others being run through local organisations or simply committees of volunteers. There were 41,300 associations across England and Wales in total. New war loans were announced with great poster campaigns – taking over from the 1914–15 recruiting effort in occupying public space. The loan launched in 1917 saw placards erected around the base of Nelson's Column, urging people to go and invest.

Another promotional tool was to display war weapons. In 'Business Men's Week' in March 1918, over £75 million was raised as five tanks visited London boroughs. Approximately £65 million of that total was raised in the City and Westminster, skewing the London figures somewhat, but the totals for the other areas show the impact of the tanks. Of the five places visited by tanks on 11 March, three raised over £200,000 (Islington, Battersea and Lewisham), with Tottenham also raising £121,000 and Willesden £90,000. These figures for that one day dwarf the totals for those places in the previous six days: £55,000 in Islington, £31,000 in Lewisham, £30,000 in Tottenham, £19,600 in Battersea, and £16,400 in Willesden.

A nurse from Mile End hospital hammering a shilling's worth of nails into an 'Iron Hindenburg' in Stepney for charity.

Captured German weapons were displayed prominently in London, here on Horse Guards Parade.

A subtle reminder of the 1917 war loan on the plinth of Nelson's Column.

In October 1918, London's 'Feed the Guns Week' again called on people to buy war bonds and war savings certificates. Over £31 million was raised, but this time about two-thirds of it came from the City and a greater contribution from the public. A central feature was a 'War Bonds village' in Trafalgar Square: a mock-up of a ruined Belgian village. When people bought their certificates, they were stamped in the modified breech of a captured German gun – hence 'feed the guns'. Other boroughs held their own 'gun days', where captured German guns were stationed outside the Town Hall or a prominent church, while

Alexandra Day in London, June 1916: wounded soldiers buy flowers for charity.

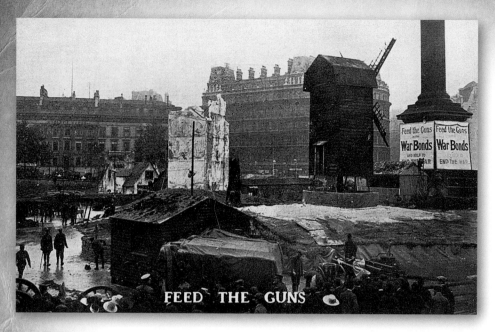

FEED THE GUNS

The fountains disappeared under landscaping, and the statue of General Gordon under a wrecked building.

a 'Wandering Gun' travelled around the City of London. Lambeth's 'gun day' raised £208,525, Battersea's £129,465, Fulham's £180,000 and Hornsey's £100,320. At the close of the week, the big guns went off to Birmingham for the 'Feed the Guns Week' there. A set of captured German guns remained in Central London, lined up along the Mall.

6

ARMISTICE AND PEACE

The fighting on the Western Front ended at 11 a.m. on 11 November 1918, and news of the Armistice immediately spread through London. Guns were fired to announce the occasion in Central London; in Croydon, the air-raid warning maroons were fired, followed by the all-clear bugle calls; the Union Flag was run up the flagpoles of the Town Hall and churches simultaneously. In the City of London, 'Within a minute the central streets were packed from side to side with wildly cheering crowds' and the buildings sprouted flags and decorations.

Outside Buckingham Palace, 5,000 people gathered within five minutes. At 11.15, the king appeared on the balcony before a large and vociferous gathering. Christopher Addison, by then Minister for Munitions, described the scene in Westminster:

> ... not only the inhabitants of the Government Offices, but as it seemed, the whole of London simultaneously 'downed' tools and rushed into the streets – taxicabs, motors, lorries, buses and vehicles of every description were commandeered by joyful crowds, driven up and down – cheering whistling, singing, rejoicing.

That evening, Vera Brittain was outside the Admiralty building on Whitehall, where 'a crazy group of convalescent Tommies were collecting specimens of different uniforms and bundling their wearers into flag-strewn taxis; with a shout they seized two of my companions and disappeared into the clamorous crowd, waving flags and shaking rattles.'

It was not quite a day of universal joy, though. While many could 'down tools', nurses and doctors still had work to do: Claire Tisdall and her colleagues had to transport the newly arrived wounded soldiers from the train stations to London's hospitals, hampered by the enormous crowds. For others it was the thought of what, or whom, they had lost that prevented it being a day for celebration. At the moment the guns were fired, Georgina Lee's friend, Florence Younghusband, was on a bus:

> In front of her were two soldiers, one with his face horribly scarred. He looked straight ahead and remained stonily silent; the other just bowed his head in his hand and burst out crying. The omnibus conductress dropped into the vacant seat next to Florence, leant her head to her shoulder and cried too. 'I lost my man two months ago, I *can't* be happy today', she murmured.

Likewise, Vera Brittain simply wanted to be alone, realising that the young men she cared about and had wanted to share her future with were gone.

Elsewhere across London, crowds gathered in public places. Mayors made speeches from the steps or balconies of their Town Halls. The festivities were not as extensive beyond Westminster and the West End, but many Londoners had streamed across the capital to be part of that crowd (around 100,000 are estimated to have taken to the streets to celebrate the Armistice). The king and queen's visit to the East End on 12 November was described as a 'return visit' after so many residents had come to Westminster the previous day.

The celebrations in Central London continued every evening for the rest of that week. Addison noted that 'crowds filled the streets from Trafalgar Square as far as Waterloo Bridge, still dancing and singing. Thanks perhaps to the still prevailing liquor restrictions, I do not remember myself seeing anybody who appeared to be drunk, although no doubt, like most other rules that week, the Closing Hour Regulations were a good deal disregarded.'

Despite this description of calmness, the *Daily Express* described a 'pandemonium' on 12 and 13 November, with 'rivers of people' and 'whirlpools of dancers', accompanied by concertinas, cornets, tambourines, wooden rattles and singing. On the 12th, a bonfire was lit on Trafalgar Square against the base of Nelson's Column; it was started at around 10 p.m. and fuelled by wooden roadblocks from the nearby roads. A temporary wooden structure in the

Rejoicing crowds filled the streets of central London. Buses and cars were commandeered to assist the celebration.

square was burned to the ground, and later one of the captured German guns that lined the Mall was added to the flames! The square was full of people setting off fireworks and crackers. Another bonfire was lit in Piccadilly Circus, fuelled by advertising hoardings from the Pavilion theatre. On the 13th, a number of German guns went missing. 'One gun was taken for a riotous joy-ride on a great motor-lorry' and disappeared 'along the Strand towards the East End trailing a "Buy War Bonds" banner', according to the *Express*. Others were pulled by hand and abandoned nearby; many appeared in Trafalgar Square, one making it as far as Piccadilly Circus. Just before midnight, the gates of Admiralty Arch were closed to try to stop the departure of more of the weapons. Another bonfire was lit in Trafalgar Square, near the end of Cockspur Street. Some soldiers fetched another captured German gun, which was again added to the fire while the crowd cheered.

The Return of Peace

The Great War cost the United Kingdom 723,000 lives and the other nations of the Empire nearly 200,000; France lost 1.3 million and Russia 1.8 million. The Allies' war dead numbered 5.4 million and the Central Powers' 4 million, half of them German and a million Austro-Hungarian. To many, the war is seen as the start of the modern age, of the 'short twentieth century' that ended with the fall of the Berlin Wall in 1989. The war saw the end of the Russian, German, Austro-Hungarian and Ottoman empires, creating new countries in Eastern Europe and the Middle East, and British Foreign Secretary Arthur Balfour's 1917 declaration that a national homeland for Jewish people should be created in Palestine was a step towards further change in the Middle East. The 1917 Russian Revolutions had brought the world's first Communist government, while the war also helped to establish the United States of America as the predominant world economic power. The UK lost most of the island of Ireland in 1922, but the British Empire reached its greatest extent.

Almost immediately after the Armistice, elements of normal life returned. The illuminated clock on Croydon Town Hall glowed again in the night sky, Big Ben sounded again after four years of silence and the Trafalgar Square fountains were switched back on. Troops began to arrive back from the war almost immediately. Prisoners of war were the first to arrive, many returning home before Christmas 1918. The demobilisation of British troops picked up speed during 1919; by October, the army had shrunk from 3.8 million men to 1 million, many of those already back in the UK. The majority of London's servicemen and women were back by late 1919. The number of male voters in Greater London who were registered as absent on war service fell from 633,000 in 1918 to 222,000 in mid-1919.

There were still many thousands who were not home, however. Some were serving in the army of occupation in Germany; others were still on the Western Front, clearing up the battlefields in labour units or working for the graves registration units attempting to identify the Empire's war dead and ensure they were properly buried. Others were still fighting. War continued through the winter of 1918/19 for men in the British forces at Archangel, fighting against the Bolsheviks in the Russian Civil War, and in 1919 an Afghan War began. One London unit, the 25th London Cyclists, had been based in India throughout the war, but found itself on the frontline in Afghanistan.

All too many of those who did return from the war, either at its end or discharged before November 1918, were permanently disabled or disfigured as a result of their service. Of the 6 million Britons who served, 1.2 million received war pensions for wounds that caused more than '20 per cent disability'. As historian Jay Winter notes, two-thirds of these were for disability of 30 per cent or less, which could mean the loss of fingers or toes, or the left thumb. Around 44,000 were 100 per cent disabled, having suffered 'the loss of two limbs, both eyes, both feet, or who were totally paralysed, permanently bedridden, suffering from severe facial disfigurement, lunacy, or incurable disease.' One of them was Albert Mason, a blinded ex-soldier from the Civil Service Rifles (15th Londons) who was awarded the Military Medal by the king. Walter Lambourne from Battersea, meanwhile, had spent only six days in the trenches in the 13th Rifle Brigade when he was wounded and lost his left leg – an 80 per cent disability.

'Shell shock' affected many veterans; it was a broad term encompassing psychological damage from the war, also termed neurasthenia. Ernest Frederick Monk, a father of eight from Lower Edmonton, enlisted in January 1915 and was blown up by an explosion near Ypres in September that year. A medical board in August 1916 found him to be 'extremely tremulous and upset by the slightest thing'; he was discharged and in January 1917 was rated as 50 per cent disabled by his neurasthenia. He reported improvement over the next two years and by 1919 was rated at 20 per cent disabled. Stagehand Lewis Havens had an even more remarkable recovery: conscripted in 1916, he lost his voice through shock while under fire at the front and was discharged from the army unable to speak in 1917. Having worked in his old job at the Hippodrome in London since that point, he recovered his voice almost three years later, after massage treatment. Others were not so lucky. William Eaglestone, a fitter's mate from Peckham, was wounded at Neuve Eglise in late 1915. Having previously been regarded hard-working, 'sober and industrious', he was now a wreck: his sleep suffered, he had lost weight, strength and memory and his knee jerked involuntarily. He was regarded as 100 per cent disabled in 1916, and by February 1918 he had not improved. 'The prognosis is hopeless,' his medical board noted.

The London to which those ex-servicemen returned to was rapidly changing, reverting from a war economy to a peacetime one. For a year from April 1919, there was a short boom in the London economy: wages, prices and the money supply all increased. By this time, the numbers of men employed in most sectors had increased: 6 per cent in industry and 44 per cent in the trams and buses; only government-run factories were shrinking, having lost 41 per cent of their male workforce and 79 per cent of their female workers by that point. The numbers of women employed across London declined as men came back: down by 23 per cent in industry more broadly and 27 per cent on the trams and buses. They made way for the men returning from the armed forces, but also for those returning to their previous occupations from war work. By the time of the 1921 census, the proportion of women employed was roughly where it had been a decade before in the county of London: 40 per cent of women over 12 were employed, compared with 39 per cent of those over 10 in 1911.

For soldiers, sailors and airmen coming back from the war, life could be very tough. In the first few years of peace, an estimated 70–80 per cent of Britain's unemployed were ex-servicemen. Times were particularly tough for those men whose military service had interrupted education or apprenticeships – those young men who were most likely to be conscripted, to serve at the front and to be killed or wounded. They came back to London without proven skills for civilian employment.

Even in the 1919–20 'boom' in London, many men struggled to find work. On 26 June 1919, all the London branches of the National Federation of Discharged Sailors and Soldiers staged a march from Cleopatra's Needle to Hyde Park, where the 10,000-strong crowd demanded that more be done to employ discharged men and that the unemployment allowance be increased from 25s to £2 (40s) per week. After the demonstration, a group broke away and descended on Parliament Square. *The Times* described the scene:

> The disorder began at the top of Victoria-street. The road was under repair, and there were missiles to hand. … [The] police were assailed with wood-blocks, and the horses of the mounted men were tripped up by scaffold poles. There was another conflict farther down Victoria-street, and the disorder reached its climax in Parliament-square … The demonstrators swept away a line of mounted policemen who had been drawn up in the square to bar their way to the House of Commons. The position looked very ugly as the crowd surged forward alongside St Margaret's Church, throwing missiles at the flying line of police. At the critical moment, a second line of mounted police, which had been held in reserve, charged the crowd and scattered it. The attitude of the crowd was so threatening that the police drew their truncheons and used them freely.

Times were harder still in the years after 1920, as the economy stagnated and unemployment increased. London never returned to the levels of poverty seen before the war, but the early years of the 1920s saw high levels of unemployment, in stark contrast to the advancement in pay and conditions achieved by many during the war and the good times those serving their country had hoped for.

Commemoration

The war left little permanent physical mark on London. The experiences of air raids, conscription and rationing were memorable and shaped expectations of the Second World War, once another conflict began to look likely. The most visible signs of the Great War in London are the war memorials erected to honour the dead of a parish, workplace, club, borough, regiment, the nation or the Empire as a whole.

As soon as the conflict was over, local communities and organisations set about planning to commemorate the conflict and those whose lives it had taken. The UK National Inventory of War Memorials lists over 3,500 memorials in London commemorating the Great War, ranging from the Cenotaph and the crosses that stand outside so many of the city's churches to pews, bells or hospital beds dedicated to the war dead; it also includes the names recorded on their parents' gravestones of

One of London's first Great War memorials, the memorial at St Botolph's-without-Bishopsgate, unveiled by the Bishop of Stepney in 1916.

sons buried thousands of miles away on the old battlefields.

Commemoration had, in fact, been going on throughout the war. Wealthy individuals paid for plaques and windows in churches to remember individuals or families, and from 1916 communal memorials began to be erected. Alongside the 'war shrines' put up across London that year, which listed those serving and the fallen, the first of London's local communal memorials to the dead of the Great War were unveiled that summer. One is outside St Botolph's-without-Bishopgate,

A 'war shrine' listing the men from Palace Road, Hackney, who were serving in the war in summer 1916.

near Liverpool Street station, and commemorates Lord Kitchener, Jack Cornwell VC, the men of the Honourable Artillery Company, and the fallen of Bishopsgate. Over in Hampstead, a Calvary was erected in honour of the local war dead at St Jude's-on-the-Hill. A few other permanent war memorials were erected during the war, including one in the East London cemetery that initially honoured the dead of the Great War of '1914–1917', but most were built after the conflict had ended, in 1919–23.

To record all the communal war memorials in London would take a vast volume in itself. A small sample of the vast number of memorials shows the range of communal commemoration in London:

- Sutton House in Homerton was, in 1914, a church room for St John's church, Hackney. On the wood-panelled wall of what was then the billiard room are engraved the names of twenty-three members of the congregation who died during the war.
- A large, ornately topped memorial in Smithfield market displays the names of 210 men who left the market to go to war and never returned.

- Outside St Michael's church on Cornhill, a winged figure dressed as a Roman soldier rises above a plaque recording that 2,130 men from offices in the parish went to war and that at least 170 lost their lives.
- In Ilford, the lone figure of a soldier stands in mourning in front of the borough's war memorial.
- In St John's Wood, a statue of St George killing the dragon serves as the St Mary-le-Bone parish memorial.
- In Finsbury, Shepherd's Bush and other districts, winged figures of Victory stand on top of plinths.
- In Sloane Square, Chelsea, stands an example of the 'Cross of Sacrifice' seen in Commonwealth War Graves Commission cemeteries around the world, adapted to serve as the borough's memorial.

Wounded soldiers at the war memorial calvary in Hampstead in 1916.

- A plaque in Cyprus Street, Bethnal Green, records the names of twenty-six men who never returned from the war; another in the Peabody buildings in Pimlico lists sixty-seven.
- In St Margaret's church in Leytonstone is a 'war shrine' that lists the names of thirty-two servicemen from nearby Chichester Road, where the shrine originally hung. Five of them died during the war.

Boroughs and districts across London invited well-known figures to unveil their war memorials – Sir Francis Lloyd, who had been the military commander of London during the war, was a popular choice, as were the commanders of British forces, such as Field Marshals Douglas Haig and Edmund Allenby. In other places, ordinary local people carried out the unveiling: in Beckenham, it was Bert Hanscombe, a local dustman and Military Medal winner who was one of nine brothers who served in (and survived) the war. In Bermondsey, a Mrs Speer, 'who lost three sons in the War performed the simple act of unveiling, and when she turned aside the great new Union Jack with its bright colours, the whole gathering throbbed with human sympathy and emotion as they realised all that this Memorial meant.'

A memorial to London troops was unveiled by the Duke of York (the future King George VI) in 1920 outside the Royal Exchange on the junction of Threadneedle Street and Cornhill. Flanked by two fully equipped soldiers and topped by the City's dragon symbol, the monument is dedicated 'To the immortal honour of the officers, non-commissioned officers and men of London who served their King and Empire in the Great War, 1914–1919'.

As a national and imperial capital, London boasts a wider range of Great War memorials than any other place in Britain. Within a short walk of Buckingham Palace are memorials erected in the 1920s and '30s to the Royal Naval Division, the Guards Division, the Rifle Brigade, the Royal Air Force, the Machine Gun Corps, the Imperial Camel Corps, and the Royal Artillery. The latter is probably the most striking: a stone howitzer on top of a plinth surrounded by four figures of artillerymen, one of them dead. It was controversial at the time, but is now acclaimed. The sculptor, Charles Sargeant Jagger, also designed the memorial to the men of the Great Western Railway Company at Paddington, a large poignant figure of a soldier reading a letter. The other London termini also host railway companies' memorials.

Other memorials mark events in London itself. A plaque adorns a building on Farringdon Road that replaced one destroyed by a Zeppelin bomb in 1915, while one of the sphinxes guarding Cleopatra's Needle still bears the scars from a bomb that fell beside it. The locations of the Eagle Hut on Aldwych and the buffet at Waterloo are also marked with plaques.

Memorial to London Troops, outside the Royal Exchange in the City.

London also contains thousands of graves of men and women who died of wounds or sickness while in London, were killed in air raids, or died soon after leaving the armed forces. Across London and Middlesex, over 8,500 are buried in 115 cemeteries, ranging from Nunhead and Greenwich cemeteries, each with over 500 war graves, to St Mary's churchyard in Acton, which holds just one. Another 11,943 are remembered on the Tower Hill memorial, which commemorates members of the merchant navy and fishing fleets who died in the war and have no known grave.

On Saturday, 19 July 1919, the nation celebrated Peace Day, after the signing of the Treaty of Versailles. The rainy weather did not deter thousands of people from flocking to Central London to watch an enormous procession of soldiers, sailors and airmen

from across the Empire and nurses and war workers, followed by a huge firework display in Hyde Park. The entire route, and much of the crowd, was decorated in the colours of the Union Flag and the flags of Britain's wartime allies. Local celebrations were held across the capital, usually focusing on ex-servicemen and children: up to 50,000 children were reportedly entertained in Wandsworth and 20,000 in Southwark. In Brixton, Islington and Croydon there were parades of soldiers and patriotic carnival floats. There was dancing into the night in Acton and on Peckham Rye Common, while an ex-servicemen's band entertained people at Finsbury, as did choirs at Chiswick and Wood Green.

The original Cenotaph was a temporary structure made of wood and papier-mâché (left), erected for the 1919 Peace Day parades. The permanent Cenotaph was unveiled on Armistice Day 1920 (right).

During the following decade, Armistice Day – the eleventh day of the eleventh month – became the focal point of remembrance of the war; over time it took on the characteristics of modern commemoration of the Great War that we know today. In earlier years, it had been an occasion for partying and celebration but gradually it became almost solely an occasion for mourning of the war dead.

The British Empire's iconic Great War memorials at the centre of this commemoration are the Cenotaph and the Tomb of the Unknown Warrior. They form a symbolic pair: the 'empty tomb', free of religious imagery, collectively commemorating all those who died in the war, and the single tomb of an individual who

The Unknown Warrior was buried in Westminster Abbey on 11 November 1920. In 1921, a permanent tombstone was laid over the grave.

could be any of those men, particularly the thousands whose bodies were never found or could not be identified.

The Cenotaph was designed by Sir Edwin Lutyens as a temporary focal point for the Peace Day parade. The original structure was made of wood and papier-mâché but proved so popular that the government decided to replace it with an almost identical permanent structure on the same spot in Whitehall. The permanent Cenotaph was unveiled by King George V on 11 November 1920. On the same day, the Unknown Warrior finished his final journey from France to Westminster Abbey, having been picked from four anonymous bodies exhumed from major battlefields on the Western Front. After arriving at Victoria Station on 10 November, the next day the body was carried on a gun carriage up to Hyde Park Corner, down Constitution Hill, past Buckingham Palace, along the Mall, past Trafalgar Square and down Whitehall, passing the Cenotaph, and into Westminster Abbey. There, accompanied by the King,

Field Marshals Haig and French, and other luminaries of the war years, he passed a guard of honour of 100 Victoria Cross winners and was laid to rest. The permanent plaque placed over the tomb a year later tells the reader:

> Beneath this stone rests the body of a British Warrior unknown by name or rank brought from France to lie among the most illustrious of the land ... Thus are commemorated the many multitudes who during the Great War of 1914–1918 gave the most that man can give, life itself, for God, for King and Country, for loved ones, home and empire, for the sacred cause of justice and the freedom of the world.

SELECT BIBLIOGRAPHY

Contemporary Works

De Ruvigny's Roll of Honour, 1914–18
National Roll of the Great War
Official History of Ministry of Munitions
Official History of Medical Services in the War
Addison, Christopher, *Four and a Half Years: A personal diary from June 1914 to January 1919*, 2 vols, (Hutchinson, 1934)
Adler, Betty, *Within the Year After* (M.A. Donohue & Co., 1920)
Allingham, Henry with Dennis Goodwin, *Kitchener's Last Volunteer: The Life of Henry Allingham, the Oldest Surviving Veteran of the Great War* (Mainstream Publishing, 2009)
Ashley, R.S., *War-diary of Private R.S. (Jock) Ashley 2472: 7th London Regiment 1914–1918* (Philippa Stone, 1982)
Bentley, E.C., *Peace Year in the City, 1918–1919* (1920)
Brittain, Vera, *A Testament of Youth: Great War Diary 1913–17* (Phoenix, 2001)
Brookes, Bernard, *A Signaller's War: Notes Compiled from My Diary 1914–1918* (lulu.com, 2012)
Bush, Eileen, *A VAD Remembers* (1971)
Dolden, A. Stuart, *Cannon Fodder: An Infantryman's Life on the Western Front, 1914–18* (Littlehampton Book Services Ltd, 1980)
Hawkings, Frank, *From Ypres to Cambrai: The 1914–1919 diary of infantryman Frank Hawkings*, edited by Arthur Taylor (TBS Ltd, 1973)

Keatley Moore, H. and W.C. Berwick Sayer, *Croydon and the Great War* (1920)

Keeling, F.H., *Keeling letters and reminiscences*, edited by E.T. (1918)

Lee, Georgina, *Home Fires Burning: the Great War diaries of Georgina Lee*, edited by Gavin Roynon (The History Press, 2006)

MacDonagh, Michael, *In London During the Great War: The Diary of a Journalist* (Eyre and Spottiswoode, 1935)

Miles, Hallie Eustace, *Untold Tales of War-time London: A Personal Diary* (Cecil Palmer, 1930)

Morriss H.F., *Bermondsey's 'Bit' in the Greatest War* (Clifton, 1919)

Noschke, Richard, *An Insight into Civilian Internment in Britain During WW1: From the Diary of Richard Noschke and a Short Essay by Rudolf Rocker* (Anglo-German Family History Society Publications, 1998)

Pankhurst, Sylvia E., *The Home Front: A Mirror to Life in England During the World War* (Ebury Press, 1932)

Peel, Mrs C.S., *How We Lived Then, 1914–1918: A sketch of social and domestic life in England during the war* (London John Lane, 1929)

Scales, Lillie, *A Home Front Diary 1914–1918* (Amberley Publishing, 2014)

Sheridan-Jones, C., *London in War-Time* (Grafton & Co., 1917)

Smith, Len, *Drawing Fire: The Diary of a Great War Artist* (Collins, 2009)

Snyder, Alice Ziska and Milton Valentine Snyder, *Paris Days and London Nights* (1921)

National Archives Papers

War Office: Recruiting Figures; Service Records
Ministry of Health: Middlesex Tribunal
Air Ministry: Records on Air Raids and Shelters

Modern Works

Adamson, John and Len Hudson (eds.) *The London Town Miscellany: Vol. 1 1900–1939* (The Alexius Press, 1992)

Britton, Tanya, *Greenfield and Perivale During World War One, 1914–1918* (2010)

Castle, Ian, *London 1914–17: The Zeppelin Menace* (Osprey Publishing, 2008)

Franks, Norman, Hal Giblin and Nigel McCrery, *Under The Guns of the Red Baron: The Complete Record of von Richthofen's Victories and Victims* (Grub Street Publishing, 2007)

Gregory, Adrian, *The Last Great War: British Society and the First World War* (Cambridge University Press, 2008)

Gregory, Adrian, *Silence of Memory: Armistice Day 1919–1946* (Berg 3PL, 1994)

Hallifax, Stuart, *Citizens at War: The Experience of the Great War in Essex, 1914–1918* (DPhil thesis, University of Oxford, 2010)

Hanson, Neil, *First Blitz* (Corgi, 2009)

Hanson, Neil, *The Unknown Soldiers: The Story of the Missing of the Great War* (Corgi, 2007)

King, John, *Grove Park in the Great War* (Grove Park Community Group, 1983)

Monger, David, *Patriotism and Propaganda in First World War Britain: The National War Aims Committee and Civilian Morale* (Liverpool University Press, 2014)

Moynihan, Michael (ed.), *Greater Love: Letters Home 1914–18* (W.H. Allen, 1980)

Panayi, Panikos, *The Enemy in our Midst*: *Germans in Britain during the First World War* (Berg 3PL, 1991)

Pennell, Catriona, *A Kingdom United: Popular Responses to the Outbreak of the First World War in Britain and Ireland* (OUP, Oxford, 2002)

Simkins, Peter, *Kitchener's Army: The Raising of the New Armies 1914–1916* (Pen & Sword Military, 1988)

Taylor, Sheila (ed.), *The Moving Metropolis: A History of London's Transport since 1800* (Te Neues, 2001)

Wilson, Trevor, *The Myriad Faces of War: Britain and the Great War, 1914–1918* (Faber & Faber, 1986)

Winter, Jay, et al: *Capital Cities at War: Paris, London, Berlin 1914–1919* 2 vols (Cambridge University Press, 1997, 2007)

Winter, J.M., *The Great War and the British People* (Palgrave Schol, 2003)

Articles

Grant, Peter, 'An infinity of personal sacrifice: The scale and nature of charitable work in Britain during the First World War', *War and Society* (2008)

Hallifax, Stuart, '"Over by Christmas": British popular opinion and the short war in 1914', *First World War Studies* (2010)

Hiley, Nicholas, '"Kitchener wants you" and "Daddy, what did YOU do in the Great War?": The Myth of British Recruiting Posters', *Imperial War Museum Review* (1997)

Papers

Imperial War Museum, department of documents: E. Bennett, C.R. Enock, M. Hardie, J. Hollister, A.W. Page and C.E. Tisdall

National Army Museum, department of documents, photographs, film and sound: R.A. Savory

Newspapers
(other than specific references in text)

The Times *New York Times*
Daily Mirror *Walthamstow Guardian*
Daily Express *Ilford Recorder*

Websites

The Long, Long Trail: www.1914–1918.net
Scarlet Finders: www.scarletfinders.co.uk
Great War Forum: http://1914–1918.invisionzone.com/forums/
Oxford Dictionary of National Biography

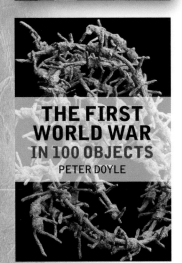

Great War Britain: The First World War at Home

Luci Gosling

After the declaration of war in 1914, the conflict dominated civilian life for the next four years. Magazines quickly adapted without losing their gossipy essence: fashion jostled for position with items on patriotic fundraising, and court presentations were replaced by notes on nursing. The result is a fascinating, amusing and uniquely feminine perspective of life on the home front.

978 0 7524 9188 2

The First World War in 100 Objects

Peter Doyle

Objects allow us to understand the experience of men and women during the First World War. This book focuses on weapons like the machine gun and vehicles such as the tank that transformed the battlefield and German submarines that stalked shipping across the seas, as well as everyday objects transformed by the harsh realities of war. Through these incredible artefacts, Peter Doyle tells the story of the First World War in a whole new light.

978 0 7524 8811 0

Visit our website and discover many other First World War books.

www.thehistorypress.co.uk/first-world-war

The History Press